F. B. Meyer

'A century ago, fine preachers attracted vast crowds. But F. B. Meyer's enduring popularity, through his devotional books, is unique. Bob Holman paints a vivid picture: preacher and evangelist, happier with the poor than the rich; remarkable social entrepreneur; and political progressive, dubbed – with Labour in its infancy – "virtually a Christian socialist". Meyer has a lot to teach our churches today.'

Rt. Hon. Stephen Timms MP

'F.B. Meyer was one of the great influences of the evangelical world in the latter 19th and early 20th century. He helped launch the then unknown D.L. Moody for his first evangelistic mission in the UK, was himself a famous Holiness preacher on both sides of the Atlantic, played a role in the Welsh Revival of 1904, wrote a number of books and was a firm believer in social action alongside evangelistic outreach. Bob Holman has done a service in bringing this remarkable character to life again, and his story will encourage, challenge and stretch us in a day when we need to rediscover men and women of this caliber who left the world a better place.'

Charles Price, Senior Pastor, The People's Church, Toronto

'For too long the figure of F. B. Meyer has been shrouded in obscurity. Yet here is a man who, in his day was committed to preaching the gospel in its fullness and expressing the gospel in all its beauty. One of the outstanding bible teachers of his day, his devotional books continue to bless the church, yet he had a great heart for the poor and marginalised. He was no pious mystic cut off from the realities of poverty or injustice. He was thoroughly biblical in his theology and radical in his actions. Bob Holman has done us a great service in bringing him to the attention of a new generation.'

Dr. Liam Goligher, Senior Minister, Duke Street Church, Richmond

'A riveting portrayal of the life of a great British preacher presented through the filter of Bob Holman, an evangelical sociologist who lived for years in Glasgow's Easterhouse Estate. With no sacrifice of scholarship, in a highly readable volume, Professor Holman irrefutably demonstrates that Meyer's social concerns were a valid outworking of the Gospel which far from diluting the message gives it credibility. A timely book!'

Rev Dr. Tony Sargent, Principal,
International Christian College, Glasgow

F. B. Meyer

*'If I had a hundred lives,
they should be at Christ's disposal.'*

Bob Holman

CHRISTIAN
FOCUS

As a child, Bob Holman endured the London blitz and evacuation. After university, he worked as a child care officer before entering academic life. He left his post as professor of social policy at the university of Bath to start a community project on a council estate. After ten years, he and his wife moved to the Easterhouse housing scheme in Glasgow to undertake neighbourhood work for 17 years. He has now retired and helps mind two grandsons. His books include *The Evacuation*(1995) and *Faith in the Poor*(1998), published by Lion. Bob is a member of Easterhouse Baptist church.

ISBN 1-84550-243-4
ISBN 978-1-84550-243-0

© Bob Holman

10 9 8 7 6 5 4 3 2 1

Published in 2007
by
Christian Focus Publications, Ltd.,
Geanies House, Fearn, Ross-shire,
IV20 1TW, Great Britain.

www.christianfocus.com

Cover design by Danie Van Straaten

Printed and bound by
Nørhaven Paperback A/S, Denmark

CONTENTS

Introduction

Several years ago, Stephen Timms MP suggested I write about F. B. Meyer. Who? All I knew was that Meyer had been a Baptist minister in Victorian times, a holiness preacher and that some of his devotional books were still in print.

At the time, I was fully involved with a community project in Easterhouse, Glasgow, but I did seek out W. Y. Fullerton's biography of Meyer, written soon after he died in 1929. I discovered that, at his death, *The Daily Telegraph* called him 'The Archbishop of the Free Churches.' In 1899, the *New York Observer* had written, 'He has an international fame and his services are constantly sought by churches over the wide and increasing empire of Christendom.'

Later I was at a meeting with the Revd Steve Chalke at the Christian organisations Faithworks and Oasis, just opposite the North Lambeth underground station in London. They are located in a church which was built to replace the much larger Christ Church, damaged by bombing during the war. Its cafe contains part of the pulpit of the former church and displays a brass plate with the names of previous ministers, including that of F. B. Meyer. When I mentioned my interest to Steve, I discovered that not only had it been Meyer's church but it contained some of his documents, which I call the Christ Church Archives. The numerous materials persuaded me to write a book about Meyer.

Given the continuing sales of Meyer's books, it is surprising that so little has been written about him since his death. Chester Mann, like Fullerton, knew Meyer and also quickly produced a book in 1929 which gives attention to Meyer's friendship with the American evangelist, Dwight Moody, and his preaching tours in the USA. Since then, the fullest study in Britain has been Ian Randall's excellent one of 2003. Any renewed interest in Meyer owes much to Randall.

The books by Fullerton, Chester Mann and Randall tend to be thematic in approach; that is, they focus on the major topics in Meyer's life like his Keswick ministry, his missionary interests and his Nonconformity rather than on a chronological narrative. I have opted for the latter and I attempt to incorporate his major issues as the story of his career and life unfolds.

What is known about Meyer concentrates on his writings and preaching. His social involvement tends to be less well-known. At the 1975 Keswick convention, Billy Graham spoke about the great social reformers of the Keswick Victorian era such as Dr. Barnardo, Lord Shaftesbury and General Booth. Almost as an afterthought, he added F. B. Meyer 'who was not able to do much in expressing his social concern, but he did what he could.' In fact, Meyer was consumed by a desire to reach the masses and to draw working class people into the church. He established a myriad of social welfare agencies to help those who suffered social distress. Eventually, he tried to persuade politicians to take action and identified closely with a political party – actions which caused some to criticise him. The Christ Church Archives have enabled me to show in detail both his spiritual and social ministries. The range of Meyer's activities is astonishing: preacher, pastor, writer, social activist, free church leader, Baptist president, advocate for missionary work and more. In his last years, he declared, 'If I had a hundred lives, they should be at Christ's disposal.' At times, it seemed as though he was living a hundred lives.

Meyer came from a conventional, middle class Victorian background and experienced no dramatic conversion. He was not a distinguished scholar and not a dramatic orator. His slight figure and retiring manner meant that he did not stand out in a crowd. Yet he drew crowds by the thousands, wrote books which sold by the millions, and attracted working class people. This study will try to identify the reasons for his achievements.

I must thank some of the many people who have helped with this book. Stephen Timms, who both suggested it and wrote the foreword. Steve Chalke, Malcolm Duncan and their colleagues who always took an interest. Dr. Tony Sargent, the principal of the International Christian College in Glasgow, both for allowing me to use the college library and for introducing me to William MacKenzie of Christian Focus Publications. Ian Randall put me in touch with Judy Powles, the librarian at Spurgeon's College, who could not have been more helpful. I received valuable information from Colin and Ann Broomfield, Andrew Jolly, Enid Measures, Mick Popplewell and Alec Porter.

As always, my wife Annette has supported me. She has lived with Meyer for two years – she even sees his photo on waking. I often tell her about Meyer and, looking at some of his photos, she asked, 'Was he a bit vain?' Perhaps he was. Meyer had his faults and I do not wish to portray him as a plaster saint.

Lastly, I seem to have met F. B. Meyer. He has helped and strengthened me. His words have often been relevant to my needs. Like many people over a hundred years ago, I give thanks for him.

Bob Holman
Glasgow

1

CALLED TO THE MINISTRY
1847–1870

'The simple faith of my boy'

A young boy, new to a public school, was bullied by older pupils. They made him promise to bring them some foreign stamps the next day – or else. He hardly knew what foreign stamps were, let alone how to get them. That evening he asked God for them but they were not on his pillow in the morning. Before leaving for school, he asked his father if he had any. To his surprise, father picked up some letters that had just arrived from abroad and gave him the stamps. The boy, Frederick Brotherton Meyer, was convinced both that God had answered his prayers and that he had chosen him to serve God in a special way.

Childhood

Frederick Brotherton Meyer was born in Clapham, London on 8 April 1847. His family called him Freddy and his mother, Anne, sometimes used Fritz, which he disliked. As an adult, he was frequently known as the Revd F. B. Meyer, Dr. Meyer, after he received an honorary doctorate, or just F. B. Meyer. I will use Freddy, F. B. Meyer, Meyer or Dr. Meyer as is appropriate to the text.

His birth certificate puts his father's occupation as 'Gentleman'. He found himself in an affluent and conventional Victorian family. His ancestors were German, with John Meyer, a sugar refiner, moving from Worms to London in the eighteenth century. His son, also John, became a partner in a flourishing city firm and his son, Frederick, a successful merchant whose boy is the subject of this book. Business interests also predominated on his mother's side. Freddy's maternal grandfather, Henry Sturt, had risen to become head of a great London firm, Wood and Sturt. Between them, the relatives conveyed business skills which Freddy later displayed in his capacity to organise and manage churches and Christian agencies.

Freddy's middle name of Brotherton derived from a close friend of his parents, Joseph Brotherton, the Liberal MP for Salford. Amongst the Christ Church Archives is a newspaper cutting dated 9 August 1856, in which a column and a half is devoted to the 'Inauguration of the Brotherton Statue.' It reported that this memorial to the late MP had been paid for by public subscription and erected in Peel Park. Tributes were paid by political and religious leaders. One praised Brotherton 'For what he had done for the lower classes.' Another said that he had possessed 'the most extensive toleration for the religious beliefs of others.' Brotherton had been a progressive politician, sympathetic towards the extension of the franchise. It is worth noting that, by his teens, Freddy identified with the Liberals and the reform movement.

Meyer had a happy childhood. Writing in adulthood, he recalled the summer days spent on Clapham Common playing amidst the gorse, followed by games of cricket 'as exciting as any that ever drew crowds to Lord's.'

The boy's father and mother were devoted parents to their son and three daughters. They were also sincere Christians who originally worshipped at Clapham Congregational Church and then at Bloomsbury Chapel, which was opened in 1848 as a leading Baptist church (and continues to this day). Its minister was Dr. William Brock, and Freddy later recalled being gripped by his fervent preaching.

Mrs Meyer was particularly concerned for the spiritual welfare of her children. The three daughters, none of whom married, grew to be strong evangelicals and were members of Pembury Free Church in Kent, where Ada Meyer became both an elder and church secretary. There was a fourth daughter, although Mrs Meyer makes no mention of her. Writing in 1895, Meyer does refer to the death of a baby sister. Mrs Meyer gave most attention to Freddy's spiritual growth. The Christ Church archives contain thirty-five handwritten pages entitled 'Early Life of Fritz. Notes by his fondly attached mother,' in which she describes several incidents. For instance, for 22 February 1852, when Freddy was nearly five, she tells how, after reading to him from a Christian book, she said, 'I think, Freddy, you ought to ask God to give you His Holy Spirit to make you good.' She continued, 'Whilst at his prayers that same Sunday evening, without my reminding him he prayed – "Put Thy Holy Spirit in me to make my heart good like Jesus Christ was."'

When he was seven and a half, she wrote, 'On coming from Chapel on Sunday after hearing Mr. Brock, Freddy said, "I have made up my mind what I shall be – I shall be a minister like Mr. Brock."'

His mother was not the only woman to influence Freddy's Christian growth. His maternal grandmother, Anne Sturt, had been a Quaker who visited the inmates of Newgate Prison, where she worked with Elizabeth Fry. After she married Henry Sturt in Lambeth Parish Church in 1820, she was officially disowned by the Society of Friends, but she cheerfully continued to worship and live as a Quaker. In 1856, when recovering from an illness, she wrote a poem about 'my little grandchild, Freddy Meyer, moving softly about my sick-bed'. Meyer later said that her early training as a Quaker gave 'a quiet dignity and charm to her character, an independence of outward formalities, a certain strength and spirituality of tone which made her unlike most others'. Meyer's early biographer, William Young Fullerton, suggests that Meyer inherited 'the Quaker simplicity of his grandmother'. This may be fanciful, although as an adult he did adopt a modest life-style. More likely, he would have been impressed by her stories of the notorious Newgate Prison and years later one of his major social welfare outreaches was to prisoners in Leicester jail.

Schooling

While growing spiritually, young Freddy did not neglect his studies. Unlike some affluent, middle class families, the Meyers did not send him to boarding school and, instead, he attended Oberlin House, a school in West Brixton. Meyer retained a small certificate, dated December 1855, which states, 'This certificate of attention to his studies and good conduct is cheerfully presented by Mr. Wilkins to Master Freddy Meyer.' He seemed happy at school and home and, as an adult, wrote about his childhood saying, 'I believe a man can bear any losses, any sorrow if he has in the background of his mind the beautiful picture of a Christian home. My whole life is embosomed in lovely associations connected with my childhood in Clapham.'

But Freddy was soon to leave Clapham. Aged nine, his parents moved to Brighton. One of his sisters was in poor health and it was considered that she would benefit from the climate of the south coast. He was sent, as a day boy, to the public school, Brighton College. A quiet boy, Freddy had to endure ragging and bullying, as noted in the stamp incident at the beginning of this chapter. He was also brave and determined; he survived the attacks without complaint and wrote warmly about the paper chases, the athletics, and exploring the cliffs. No mention is made of academic achievements.

A few years later, when Freddy was about fifteen, his father suffered severe losses on the stock exchange. He was removed from Brighton College and, for a year, lived with his aunt and uncle, Mr. and Mrs George Gladstone, in Clapham. Mr. Gladstone was a close friend of James Baldwin Brown, a Congregational minister who had written a controversial book called *The Fatherhood of God*, describing God as the loving Father of all. Some evangelicals replied that God was the Father of believers only. A later pamphlet, perhaps written by Meyer or, at least strongly influenced by him, stated that Freddy 'had a passionate admiration for Baldwin Brown, and still recalls his slight, spare figure, beautiful face, and exquisitely modulated voice. From Baldwin Brown he learned to take a broad and generous view in theological matters, and never forgot the rule of charity.'

Meanwhile, Freddy completed his schooling at the school of a Mr. Mason in Denmark Hill and returned to be with his family at their new home in Streatham. The Meyers were by no means poor but certainly not as wealthy as before. Meyer later saw the positive side of his changed circumstances and recalled about himself, 'It brought out all the lad's self-restraint in order to save needless expense; it took away the temptation to expect from others a deference due rather to wealth than worth.' The family decided not to worship at Bloomsbury, although they maintained contact with Dr. Brock, and attended New Park Road Baptist Chapel in Brixton, which was nearer. It was here that Freddy was baptised on 2 June 1864 at the age of sixteen by the Revd David Jones. His baptism was by full immersion not the sprinkling of a baby. Freddy was to become a strong advocate of this kind of baptism and practised it even when he ministered in non-Baptist churches.

Meyer's Britain
To put Meyer in his context, it is necessary to know something about the Britain in which he was born and bred and grew up. In his classic history of the period, Sir Robert Ensor states, 'It was one of the most religious (countries) that the world had known.' The religion, of course, was overwhelmingly Christian, although it divided into Roman Catholics and Protestants, with the latter having not just the Church of England and its counter-parts in Scotland, Wales and Ireland but also numbers of different Nonconformist denominations. One of the fastest growing of the latter in the first half of the nineteenth century were the Baptists, howbeit still a small percentage of the population as a whole. However, in the poorest parts of the country, church attendance was low. In Meyer's lifetime, traditional Christian belief came under attack from a small but significant minority who questioned the historical truths of parts of the Bible and, in some cases, proclaimed atheism.

Victorian Britain witnessed the growth of industrial, commercial and financial organisations which made some citizens very wealthy and provided skilled working class people with improved wages and life styles. There was another side. The decline of agriculture, the drift to towns, the growth of the population, led to multitudes of people in very lowly paid and intermittent jobs or no jobs at all. They tended to cram into slum conditions characterised by overcrowding, ill-health and hunger.

The suffering of the masses is well documented. A few years before Meyer was born, Frederick Engels completed his classic *The Condition of the Working Class in England.* His collection of statistics, his own astute observations and his readiness to meet, mix with and learn from poor people enabled him to show that unskilled workers faced gruelling work conditions, along with wages too small to allow them to save. When unemployment came, they could not pay the rent nor feed their families. The poorest, if not sleeping on the streets, would be fortunate to have one damp room per family. Children were particularly at risk and in Manchester over fifty-seven percent of children of working class parents died before they were five.

A very different but just as moving account was written by A. L. Calman in 1875, based on the diaries of John Ashworth of Rochdale, who had himself experienced poverty and later ministered to the poor. For instance, one day in October 1862 he had written, 'Was called this morning to pray with a dying child in the gank – a bag of shavings, a bed of rags. A boy in his shirt, three drunken women, a child in brain fever; all in one room, with one window; a dreadful sight.'

Much better known was the later work of the social scientist, Charles Booth, who in 1889 started his series on *The Life and Labour of the People of London* which led to his figure that thirty percent of the inhabitants of London were in poverty. General William Booth's *In Darkest England and the Way Out* gave horrifying details of the extent and nature of poverty.

When skilled working men experienced unemployment or sickness, they sometimes had membership of trade unions or friendly societies to tide them over. For the unskilled and unemployed, there was little state help. John Bird, the Archbishop of Canterbury between 1848 and 1862, drew upon the economists Adam Smith and Thomas Malthus to argue, in a number of publications, that state intervention was harmful and would encourage the poor to be lazy. This is not to say that state involvement did not grow in the nineteenth century. Reform of sanitation, the growth of services by local authorities and the extension of the franchise are examples of state action. But little statutory provision was made for the poor. As the social historians Young and Ashton put it, 'Old age, sickness, unemployment, widowhood were still terrors to the poor.' Churches and voluntary societies helped some but, for the majority of poor people, the only option to starvation was the Poor Law with its dreaded workhouse, where families were split asunder and conditions were harsh. In 1904, when Meyer was at his height, my grandfather, a bricklayer in Barking, became unemployed. He wrote, 'There being no unemployment insurance at that time, the five pounds we had saved was soon expended.' The family was saved from the workhouse because their landlady allowed them to stay free in their rooms. Eventually he got a job on the railways but, tragically, was run over by a train and had to have a leg amputated.

With poverty came crime, drink and prostitution. Of course, these evils were not the preserve of the poor, but the affluent could do them in greater secrecy. With alcohol cheap and available, it was used by poor people as an escape from intolerable conditions and lives. For some, crime and prostitution were the only ways of obtaining money.

Called to the Ministry

Britain was also a society with rigid social classes. It was not just that the wealthy landowners lived apart from the mill owners and shopkeepers, but also that the latter kept their social distance from the poor – except to use them for menial tasks. Thus Freddy Meyer would not have played with or even spoken to children at the hard end of society. It was not a desire to help the poor that motivated him to enter the ministry, and it was only as he grew older that his heart was opened to them.

As a small child, Freddy had been attracted to being a minister. Matters came to a head in his sixteenth year. In the Christ Church Archives is a statement by him dated 14 March 1864, a few months before he was baptised. He puts down the reasons why he felt called to the ministry. It appears to be Freddy putting his thoughts on paper to clarify his own mind. Or it could be his notes on what he intended to say to his father about his future career. He wrote,

> I have had a wish to be a minister for long, How came that wish? God must have put it in my heart... It can not be for earthly advantage for I have good prospects in life.

> First I am saved myself and should wish to save others from everlasting, eternal death. second I should like to help His kingdom through the word. third I think that God has really put this motive in my heart, though it is very cold as yet... fourth I would copy Christ and live nearer to Him and serve Him more and lay up treasures in heaven all which I can not if I serve Mammon too.

The interview with his father took place when Freddy was sixteen and three quarters. Mrs Meyer must have been informed in detail by her husband for she records it in his words as follows,

> We have often talked as to different lines of business, professional pursuits, such as law or medicine; but never ever spoken of the highest and noblest pursuit of the Christian ministry. I was therefore the more taken by surprise when ... with great modesty and deep feeling (he) introduced the subject of the future. ... He had for years past, indeed as long back as he could remember, had a wish for the ministry. ... He knew that he had nothing to gain in a temporal point of view, but the contrary – I did not fail during our conversation to impress upon him the entire surrender which a decision

for the ministry involved of all worldly advantage – and especially Baptists – there was nothing of that kind to look forward to, but the contrary, and that in respect of myself and looking at my age, and the fact of my being burdened with two young partners, I could not in the nature of things hope to leave much behind for his dear Mother, himself and sisters. But all this seemed to have no effect, except a reiteration of his former expression that there seemed to him to be nothing else worth living for and that he would leave all the rest in better hands.

I confess I felt abashed before the simple faith of my boy, and cheerfully approved his decision.

Despite their approval, Freddy's parents advised him to gain experience in business before entering the ministry. He took a post at Allan Murray, tea merchants – in later life, Meyer laughingly considered himself an expert on tea and would often make it at church gatherings. He showed a good head for business and could have continued with the firm. Outside of work and family, he participated in a debating society and sometimes went to hear the great preachers of the time such as Charles Spurgeon.

The young Meyer enjoyed commercial life but nothing could shake his resolve to be a minister. He approached the Revd Jones and his mother recorded in her lengthy epistle,

About the beginning of the year 1866, Fritz requested Mr. Jones to permit him to try his power in preaching, as he still felt called to the work, and wished to test himself. He preached with so much satisfaction to Mr. Jones, that on mentioning his pleasure to Mr. Brock, he most kindly wished him to preach in the mission hall. Mr. Brock, Mr. Jones and Mr. McCree being present and all pronounced he had qualifications for the ministry.

The Seven Dials Mission was run by Bloomsbury Baptist Church under George McCree, a lay worker noted for his work amongst poor people. He subsequently moved to Borough Road Chapel where he helped costermongers to purchase their own barrows. Meyer's contacts with McCree may have been the beginning of his eventual determination to reach and help those outside the church.

Encouraged by their approval, Freddy applied to Regent's Park College, which trained men for the Baptist ministry, passed a preliminary examination and entered in October 1866 aged nineteen, the youngest student in the college. The principal was Joseph Angus, a distinguished scholar who linked the college with London University.

Regent's Park College

Freddy's time at college overlapped with a correspondence he maintained with 'Herbert'. In the Christ Church Archives are thirty-one letters written by Freddy Meyer to this man. How this bundle of hand-written letters to his friend finished up in the archives is not known. Possibly Herbert's parents returned them after his death.

Herbert was Herbert Allport. The letters are mostly undated but reference to political events of the time makes it clear that they were written between 1865 and 1869, that is they commenced just before Freddy started at college and continued until he was about to leave. Who was Herbert? My guess is that he was a school friend, probably at Brighton College. They make mention of one other former school friend who had come to London to study medicine at Guy's Hospital. Like Freddy, Herbert was making his way in business and, also like him, he wanted to do something different, namely get into Oxford University. They both lived in the same part of London, knew each other's families and would go out together for their leisure. The value of the letters is the clues they give about Freddy's early interests and views.

The first letter, written while Freddy was still employed at the tea merchants, broke the news to Herbert that he was going to be a minister. He wrote,

... for friendship's sake I do not want to conceal from you, or in fact from anyone else, the decision to which I have come. So to be frank I have decided my future career. I am going, with help from above, to be a minister of the gospel. Now I can imagine your astonishment but it is a fact.

I am going to preach no sermon, but that is the case stated. I know you do not quite agree with me about these matters but I still hope there will be no intermission of our correspondence or schism in our friendship.

Herbert certainly did not hold the same views about Christianity and subsequent letters – and no doubt conversations when they met – were often about religion. Herbert could not see why the Bible was superior to the Koran and in a letter, by which time he was at college, Freddy argued that the Bible's accurate recording of miracles, the fulfilment of prophecies, and the testimonies of thousands of people showed it to be a unique book. On another occasion, he tried to explain why it was necessary for Jesus to die for our sins and why allowing His son to die was consistent with God's love for Him.

In a following letter, he outlined his faith. He believed the Bible as God's revelation: that conversion depended upon belief in heart and mind: that mankind was justly condemned for sin but God's infinite love resulted in Jesus coming to earth and 'that his death is accepted by Infinite justice as the basis of reconciliation between man and God'. This gospel remained with him all his life. It is not known whether Herbert was persuaded.

Freddy was a staunch evangelical yet the letters reveal that he was prepared to go to a Roman Catholic church, an act which would have been unacceptable to many conservative evangelicals. In one of the few dated letters, 27 December 1865, he told his friend, perhaps tongue in cheek, 'Like a good Catholic, I went on Monday to the Roman Catholic Cathedral, Southwark, to hear mass. They played Mozart's twelfth mass splendidly.'

Freddy and Herbert also disagreed about politics. The former was a Liberal, the latter a Conservative. Freddy admired the Liberal politician, William Gladstone, and informed Herbert that he had been to hear him speak. These were years of turmoil about whether the right to vote should be extended. Less than one million men in England and Wales could vote. Generally the Liberals wanted a moderate extension while the Conservatives were opposed. Freddy appeared even more radical for he waxed enthusiastically about the MP, John Bright of the Reform League, who wanted more extensive changes. He wrote excitedly about demonstrations by the Reform League and asked, 'What do you think of our down-trodden masses now – you try to dam up the river, but it will soon burst over your petty objectives and carry you all away?'

There followed the famous reversal in 1867 when the Conservatives, led by Disraeli in the Commons, suddenly pushed through their own reform bill. This must explain Freddy's written outburst, 'My dear Conservative friend, it seems that you have out heroded Herod or rather outdone Liberals in the most advanced politics ever.'

Probably the young student would have liked to attend more meetings but he had to put off some outings with Herbert to concentrate on his studies. Even so, on one occasion he had to write, 'I failed in my 1st B.A. over what I thought myself pretty safe – doubtless it is intended as a lesson for me.'

It was not all study. Freddy told his friend how he participated in college debates. He also appears to have played football, to have followed county cricket and to have enjoyed skating in nearby Regent's Park. Indeed, he was present during a tragedy when the ice cracked and some skaters were drowned, 'the sight I shall never forget'.

Freddy had a playful side which came out in his gentle teasing of Herbert about his prowess as a lady's man. While they were both working in the city, it seems that they had sometimes gone on walks together to view the young ladies. From college, Freddy asked, 'How are you getting on in your Saturday promenade? I hope you continue to maintain your prestige. Really it is perfectly hopeless to attempt to walk down the Palace with you seeing that directly you appear – well, I will not say what. Only I really must bring young ladies of my own from a distance, as no rival can stand his ground with you.' It appears that Herbert had more success with the opposite sex than his friend.

The letters apparently stopped when Meyer left college while Herbert progressed to Oxford.

The Herbert letters are not the only source of information about Freddy's college days. One of the ministerial students was John Whitaker who later recalled of Freddy,

Tall, slim, fair-looking, he had far more the appearance of a bright boy in the early teens than of a young man on the verge of twenty. ... He had a big heart even then. He was most considerate and kind. He could not refrain from smiles or restrain loud laughter.'

He had a particular chum in Herbert Smith (not the Herbert of the letters). They would often read together from Tennyson, Keats and Shelley and other poets. Freddy already had a great love of literature which later came out in his sermons and publications. They also prayed together and kept in touch for the rest of their lives.

On Sundays, the students helped at outside churches. Freddy and Herbert were assigned to a small church run by a local furniture dealer. They improved attendances by introducing 'tea meetings' to which over a hundred came. Then they had to walk for an hour back to college. In his final year, Freddy went to work with a group of Baptists in Richmond which eventually became the well-known Duke Street Chapel. Years later, Freddy recalled that one of the old deacons there taught him much about preaching. He must have made an impression because the church invited him to be their minister when he left college. He consulted the Revd William Brock who, in a letter dated 28 July 1869, advised against Richmond as he would be 'saddled with setting it up'. He continued, 'What I would like for you would be a church already formed and well at work where all your strength would be expended on the ministry and the pastorate.' Meyer took his advice and declined.

By this time, Freddy – I shall now call him Meyer – had obtained his B.A. from London University, had completed the course and pondered what to do. As well as Richmond, he also refused an offer from a church in Southampton. He did not consider himself ready to have the sole charge of a church. He knew that his conventional background had not given him the width of worldly experience of some of the older students. Yet he was still convinced that God had called him to the ministry. He therefore accepted an approach to be an assistant minister at Pembroke Chapel in Liverpool. The minister there was the very experienced Revd Charles Mitchell Birrell and Meyer looked forward to learning from him. He started there on 1 January 1870. The modest young man in his early twenties could hardly have envisaged that he was to become one of Britain's leading Christian figures.

2

MAKING OF A MINISTER
1870–1874

'What an inspiration when this great and noble soul (Moody)
first broke into my life!'

Meyer started at Pembroke Chapel on the first day of 1870. The
minister, Charles Birrell, was one of the leading Baptist ministers
with connections throughout Liverpool and Britain. He was
married to the cousin of Josephine Butler, which gave him some
interest in social reform. Josephine came from a well-to-do family
but was determined to serve God amongst the socially needy.
She had moved to Liverpool in 1866 when her husband became
headmaster of Liverpool College and sought Birrell's advice on
where she might start. He suggested Brownlow Hill Workhouse,
which he often visited, and also gave her the addresses of destitute
women. This was the start of Josephine's famous work amongst
prostitutes which was to make her one of the best-known women
social reformers in Britain. In March 1870, when she nervously
first spoke from a public platform, Birrell was beside her.

Pembroke Chapel
Birrell took a great interest in Meyer, giving him advice on his
sermons, making sure that he had enough time for study, and
often taking him into his own home. Ian Randall, in his well-
documented book, describes Birrell as 'a moderate Calvinist' who
introduced the young minister to the writings of nineteenth-
century Scottish divines such as Andrew and Horatio Bonar and

Murray McCheyne. Meyer later revealed that one of his most treasured possessions was a page from McCheyne's diary and Randall adds that he was taken by McCheyne's 'combination of fervent piety and the heart of an evangelist'. Meyer must have made quick progress for, on 23 May 1870, the church passed a resolution promoting him from assistant to associate minister with a salary of £200 a year.

In later life, Meyer looked back fondly on these days and said, 'It was an honour and a privilege for me to be near to Mr. Birrell, whose saintly character was revered by all who knew him. He was an ascetic in many of his habits, making it a rule to eat less food on Friday, and spending the whole of Saturday in prayer. He had travelled much and often in the evenings his daughter Olive and his son Austin and I would gather around him and listen to his wonderful tales of foreign cities.' Meyer became good friends with Austin (or Augustine) who later became a distinguished politician.

Fullerton says that Meyer hero-worshipped Birrell and continued, 'F. B. Meyer soon became Birrellised ... imitating the methods and mannerisms of his master' and preaching in the style of Birrell. Birrell was a polished speaker who wrote out and then memorised his sermons. Fullerton considered that they reached intellects more than hearts and that Meyer had eventually to adopt a more down to earth style.

Apart from preaching, Meyer did much visiting of church members. As a student at Richmond, he had showed a flair for knocking on doors and his ease in conversations was appreciated in the homes.

It was not all work. Meyer also got down to some serious courting. On 20 February 1871, Meyer, aged twenty-three, married Miss Jane Eliza Jones (usually known as Jeannie), aged twenty-five, of Birkenhead at Trinity United Presbyterian Church in Birkenhead. It is not known how they met and the engagement could not have been a long one for Meyer had been in Liverpool for only fourteen months when they married. The marriage certificate reveals that Jeannie's father (deceased) had been a builder while the occupation of Meyer's father was recorded as gentleman. None of Meyer's relatives signed as witnesses, although one of Jeannie's did along with the Revd Birrell. In the notes she kept, Meyer's mother records the marriage but does not mention the wife by name. It may be that, in those Victorian times, Meyer's family considered he had married beneath himself.

Just under a year later, on 14 January 1872, their only child, Gertrude Hilda (usually referred to as Hilda) was born.

Fullerton, who knew the Meyers well for many years, chooses his words carefully when speaking of their marriage. He said that Meyer had been 'conquered by this lady of fascinating personality, creative imagination and undeviating will' and adds that 'for more than fifty-eight years he (Meyer) rendered to Mrs Meyer most chivalrous devotion'. The nature of their relationship will be touched upon in a later chapter.

Much as he respected Birrell, there are indications that Meyer was formulating a different concept of ministry. Birrell's intellectual sermons did not draw in working class people and Meyer seemed uneasy with a ministry which concentrated mainly on church members. Even before he went to college, the teenage Meyer had been ready to speak of his faith to work colleagues. At college, he had participated in open air evangelism and in Richmond had attempted to draw outsiders into the church. Birrell, for all his support of Josephine Butler, was not an evangelist to what Meyer called 'the masses'. He was not sure how to develop a different ministry but he was ready to move on.

York and Moody

In 1872, Birrell decided to resign because of ill-health. The church deacons made it clear that Meyer was too inexperienced to succeed to such a large church. Meyer agreed and soon accepted an invitation to Priory Street Baptist Chapel in York. He left Liverpool with the warm thanks of the church and a gift of sixty guineas. Charles Birrell remained a friend and they exchanged letters for some time.

Meyer started at York on 1 May 1872. During his first year at Priory Street, Meyer concentrated on the church's internal affairs. He had to deal with a dispute which resulted in one member being struck off the church's roll. He baptised fifteen people and his preaching drew in larger numbers. Meyer also played a full part in the Yorkshire Baptist Association. Fullerton sums up, 'But there was only a scanty record of conversions, and though he became popular he scarcely imagined himself to be successful as a minister of Jesus Christ.'

Then came Dwight Moody, whose life story is vividly told by John Pollock. Ten years older than Meyer, Moody was born in Northfield, Massachusetts in poor circumstances. With little formal education, he left home aged seventeen and soon showed his talent for making money. In Chicago he was converted and developed as an evangelist with the Young Men's Christian Association (YMCA). In 1867, Moody and his wife, Emma, made a social visit to Britain. He returned in 1872 when his down-to-earth preaching impressed those who heard him. One was the evangelical Anglican, William Pennefather, who invited him to come back and lead a mission. Henry Bewley of Dublin and Cuthbert Bainbridge of Newcastle-upon-Tyne promised financial support. Meanwhile, George Bennett of the York YMCA wrote to ask Moody to speak in York if he did come.

In 1873 Moody, his family and the singer Ira Sankey, landed at Liverpool to discover that Pennefather and Bainbridge had died while Bewley seemed to have forgotten. As Pollock puts it, 'There were no engagements, no committee, no funds.' Moody telegrammed Bennett and travelled to York where the surprised Bennett hastily arranged a few meetings. After these, they made their way to Priory Street Baptist Chapel. Pollock describes the following events,

> The starchy young minister, Frederick Brotherton Meyer, consulted by Bennett on Moody's telegram, was puzzled as to what an evangelist did that he could not do himself, being correct in doctrine, painstaking in preaching, a most worthy

young man; but with only the slightest curl of his classical nose he had invited Moody to his pulpit.

Pollock appears to over-use his imagination here. Meyer might have been a prim teenager but he was not starchy and made easy contacts with people he visited. He did not have a classical nose and there are no mentions of him curling it. Chester Mann, who knew both Meyer and Moody, has a different version. He writes that Moody and Sankey

> went to Meyer, at that time pastor of Priory Street Baptist Chapel in the city. Here they were received with open arms and accorded the most cordial welcome. And thus it came about that in F. B. Meyer's church Moody and Sankey virtually began their triumphant British tour.

Meyer and Moody walked the streets as they planned the meetings. Some went on for six hours ending with a communion service conducted by Meyer and three other ministers. Five weeks of services resulted in the professed conversions of several hundred people. Moody's tour of Britain continued until 1875, culminating at the Royal Opera House in London.

However Meyer's involvement came about, there is no doubt that it made a tremendous impression on him. Years later he wrote

> What an inspiration when this great and noble soul first broke into my life! I was a young pastor then, in the old city of York, and bound rather rigidly by the chains of conventionalism. Such had been my training, and such might have been my career. But here was revelation of a new ideal. The first characteristic of Mr. Moody's that struck me was that he was so absolutely unconventional and natural. That a piece of work had generally been done after a certain method would probably be the reason why he would set about it in some fresh and unexpected way. That the new method startled people was the greater reason for continuing with it,

if only it drew them to the Gospel. But there was never the slightest approach to irreverence, fanaticism, or extravagance; everything was in perfect accord with a rare common sense, a directness of method, a simplicity and transparency of aim, which were as attractive as they were fruitful in result.

The first ten days of his meetings were only moderately successful, and he gladly accepted my invitation to come to the chapel where I ministered, and there we had a fortnight of most blessed and memorable meetings. The little vestry there – how vividly I remember it! – was the scene of our long and earnest prayers as we knelt around the leather-covered table in the middle of the room.

Moody did not preach a different gospel from Meyer. The difference was the way he delivered it. It was in language and with illustrations which working class people could understand – often laced with humour. It was direct so that listeners thought that it was as though he was talking just to them. It was energetic as Moody walked about the pulpit and the aisles. It was passionate with Moody conveying it as the most important thing in the world. And he called for listeners to decide for Christ on the spot, often by walking to the front. Not least, Moody did not confine preaching to the church. He used public halls, concert halls, the open air, the kind of places where people felt comfortable.

Meyer was careful to explain that Moody did not create in him a desire to draw people to Christianity. Rather it was that Moody taught him how to do it. By his own example, Moody showed him how to win people for Christ. However, he did not say that he should model himself on him (Moody). Rather he said that Meyer should be himself rather than his image of the conventional minister.

Meyer perceived that people outside the church could be converted and he immediately put it into action. The membership of Priory Road increased from 114 in 1873 to 166 in 1874. Others came but did not become members. Meyer retained most of the invitations he received to pastor churches and it is noticeable that the hand-written one from Priory Street sent to him in April 1872 had made no mention of evangelism. Disagreements occurred within the church which Randall believes arose 'because some deacons did not embrace Meyer's evangelistic priorities'.

Two other outcomes emerged from Moody's explosive visit. One was a life-long friendship between Meyer and Moody. In a later chapter, attention will be given to Meyer's many visits to preach for Moody in the USA. Suffice here to record that when, shortly before Meyer's death, Fullerton visited the Bible Institute founded by Moody in Chicago, he noticed two large photos on the wall. One of Moody and one of Meyer.

The other outcome was to change Meyer's view on denominationalism. He had been a Baptist from boyhood and never considered serving in any other church. Moody had little time for denominational restrictions and would preach anywhere and co-operate with any Christians. Twenty years later, Meyer wrote of this impact of Moody at York

> There I caught a glimpse of a wider, larger life, in which mere denominationalism could have no place, and in which there was but one standard by which to measure men, namely their devotion to, and knowledge of the Son of God. Thank God I have never receded from that position, and I hope that I never shall. Whilst willing to devote my energies to those with whom my belief on one great subject necessarily allies me, yet I refuse to be a mere denominationalist, and I glory most in being a member of the one Catholic church, and the brother of all who love the Lord Jesus Christ in sincerity.

The 'one great subject' was adult baptism. Meyer never wavered in his insistence on baptising adult believers wherever he was a minister. However, his freeing himself from denominationalism did open the doors to his ministries in other churches. But this did not mean he abandoned the Baptist cause and later he became a notable president of the Baptist Union.

The meeting with Moody can be described as the first major turning point in Meyer's ministry. It confirmed his growing belief that he should take the gospel to the masses. It made him re-consider the style of his ministry. And it made him ready to co-operate with and identify with other denominations.

In 1874 Meyer left Priory Street Baptist Chapel. His mother noted, 'He remained at York till August 1874 when he was called to the church at Leicester, and after much anxious thought, he decided to accept the offer, as both his health and that of Jeannie were suffering from their residence in York.' She continued in glowing terms, 'He was very much beloved at York, and it was with sincere regret he left. When he first went to York the church was in a very low condition, but before leaving it had greatly changed, the church was nearly filled and there were many added to the church.' Meyer recorded that one morning he read of the death of Dr. Haycroft, the minister at Victoria Road Baptist Chapel in Leicester, and an inward voice said to him 'You will go to Victoria Road'. Soon after, one of the deacons from that church came to hear Meyer preach and reported favourably on him.

Meyer's decision to leave suddenly – not for the last time – surprised the church. It did not seem connected with his disagreement with a minority of deacons for the church offered to move the Meyers to a manse in a healthier part of York. Certainly, Mrs Meyer was often in poor health. Probably, also, Meyer wanted a new challenge where he could put into practice his changing concept of the ministry which put an emphasis on reaching those outside the church.

3

FROM CHURCH TO PRISON: LEICESTER
1874–1887

'Willing to be made willing'

If the four years in Liverpool and York prompted Meyer to re-think the nature of his ministry, the following thirteen years in Leicester saw him develop, practise and establish it. He went to Leicester as just another Baptist minister, he left with a growing national reputation.

'This is not a gospel shop'

Victoria Road Baptist Chapel in Leicester was well-known within the Baptist denomination and its worshippers included several wealthy families. Following the death of its minister, the church members held a meeting on 4 June 1874 and unanimously resolved to invite Meyer to be their pastor with the not inconsiderable stipend of 400 guineas a year. The document sent to Meyer stressed the importance of 'pastoral visitation' and 'attention to our young people'. There was nothing about evangelism. Meyer accepted and commenced his ministry in September of that year.

During the first month at Victoria Road, Meyer ended an address with an invitation to those who desired to become Christians to gather in the chancel at the close of the meeting. He must have been delighted when more than eighty responded. But one deacon was less than pleased and throwing up his hands cried, 'We cannot have this sort of thing; this is not a gospel shop.'

Meyer seemed taken aback by this criticism and, for a while, provided the kind of ministry the deacons wanted. His preaching attracted a larger congregation and membership increased.

His conviction that he must appeal to the masses, however, did not go away. Writing later of his Leicester years, he recalled 'meeting the long stream of operatives hurrying down the street from their brief dinner-hour, to the heart of the town, where the factories are situated.' He attributed their reluctance to enter churches to the pew system, whereby some members paid for and reserved the best seats and so emphasised the distinctions imposed by money and class. He added, 'I often wished that the time might come when I could preach regularly in a building where all the seats were perfectly open and free to all comers.'

The leaders at Victoria Road must have been sensitive to their young minister's desire to reach out in evangelism and suggested to him that, as with some other churches, a mission church should be started in a down-town area. Meyer was dubious because such a step immediately divided Christians into two classes. He began to grapple with a different concept in which the church was a hub which reached out to and then drew in people beyond itself.

Meyer shared his vision with some sympathisers within the church and some young men from other churches. This provoked criticism that he was splitting his own and other churches. The hostility became so intense that a number of ministers called on him and urged him to leave Leicester. The leaders at Victoria Road were also disturbed. As his mother recorded, 'he resigned owing to dissatisfaction of the deacons, as he wished to undertake preaching amongst the working classes.' He left the church in May 1878.

Pastor Without a Church

What were Meyer's faults to churches in Leicester, appeared as virtues to other churches. He soon received invitations from Birmingham, Derby and Sheffield.

Meyer was in a dilemma. He felt called to reach the masses in Leicester. Yet, with no job, he had no income. He was never over-concerned about money but he had a wife and a six-year-old daughter to support. He wrote a letter of acceptance to the church in Sheffield and walked from his home to post it.

Meanwhile a group who shared Meyer's vision, including a number of business men, agreed that they would back him to stay in Leicester. One was Fullerton's brother-in-law, Arthur Rust, who had also gone to post a letter and met Meyer. Meyer explained what was in his letter while Rust explained the decision of the group. Meyer kept the letter in his pocket and went home to consider. If he accepted the offer, he would further antagonise local ministers by drawing people from their churches. There was another consideration. John Howard Shakespeare was then a young man in Leicester and years later became secretary of the Baptist Union and one of Meyer's closest friends. He was to write of Meyer's back-peddling of evangelism at Victoria Road, 'Mr. Meyer weakly yielded, and has never ceased to feel that he missed one of the great opportunities of his life.' He decided he would not miss another opportunity to evangelise in Leicester and he accepted the offer.

The following Saturday the group made their plans. Services were started in the Museum Buildings – where one elderly woman supporter insisted on covering up the nude statues. The meetings were well attended but Meyer was not satisfied. Three times a week he and the team held open air meetings in Infirmary Square. Paradise Mission, the hall which Victoria Road Church had offered as a mission hall, was taken over and Fullerton recalled some sneering that Meyer had been reduced to a city missioner.

Their numbers and vision grew. In September 1878, seventy-seven constituted themselves as a church. They signed a declaration which included the intent to help the poor, 'to evangelise the great masses of our population' and with every member pledged to be a worker.

Melbourne Hall
Without being sought by public appeals, money came in for a building until £10,000 had been raised. A site was found and on 1st

July 1880, Meyer's father laid a memorial stone and the building was complete by 1881. For three years, Meyer had been a minister without a church. Now he had a huge hall in Melbourne Road – Melbourne Hall. Meyer later wrote that, up to this point, he had failed in his purposes because he was tied to

> a certain idea of the dignity of the ministerial office, which restrained me from entering freely into the life of the people and hedged me around with a reserve that hid my real self. All this, however, in God's own time and way, came to an end when, having resigned my pastorate of Victoria Church, I undertook the work which developed into Melbourne Hall, and from the first was intended to reach those masses of the people who seemed altogether beyond the ordinary means of grace.

Before long the Sunday meetings at Melbourne Hall, where all the seats were free, were drawing 1,400 worshippers. Although a hall, it was also a church with members. Indeed it was a Baptist church which became a part of the Leicestershire Baptist Association. The Sunday Schools were so large, about 2,500 scholars, that three council schools had to be rented to accommodate them. Fullerton later became the minister of Melbourne Hall and, writing after Meyer's death, he recorded that its membership was over 1,300.

The building was not used just on Sundays. During the week, there were temperance meetings, missionary gatherings, educational classes, and a coffee and reading room. Indeed, such was the pressure for space that an extension had to be added. These facilities were part of Meyer's strategy to provide recreation for young people. He pointed out that gin palaces and beer shops were always open so 'How can we expect to hold our young people, or our reclaimed working men if we only give them shelter and welcome for two or three hours on Sunday, and leave them to spend all their leisure hours just where they may?'

But had the church drawn in working class people? The original nucleus included a number of prosperous business people plus some artisans. Meyer continued to reach out through door knocking in the neighbourhood and through open air meetings in the city centre and soon he recruited about a hundred young people to hold meetings in nearby villages on Saturday afternoons. Noticeably, of the 1,400 worshippers on a Sunday about two thirds were not members, an indication that newcomers were attending. Incidentally, Meyer had glass doors fitted so that when working class people came they could look in and decide whether it suited them! He also seemed to meet with some local people before the morning service. The conclusion is that numbers of working people were attracted to Melbourne Hall and to the gospel but were not always fully integrated with the more affluent worshippers. Every activity was surrounded with prayer, starting with four prayer meetings on Saturday evening at which Meyer told participants not to pray for more than three minutes.

Waiting at the Prison Gates

Surely Meyer had fulfilled his dreams? No way. He now regarded the church as a centre or agency which had to reach out not just to evangelise working class people but also to provide services to the most needy in the community. But how? The answer came from a young girl who attended the church and told Meyer that her father was being discharged from prison the next day. She asked Meyer to meet him as she feared he would be immediately attracted to his former bad companions. The following morning, Meyer stood nervously outside the imposing Leicester Prison. Having visited a prisoner there myself, I can appreciate his feelings. He spoke through the grating and, almost to his relief, was told that the man had been transferred to another jail.

Meyer waited awhile and noticed that the first man to be discharged was taken by friends into the nearby pub. The next had no one to welcome him, hesitated, and then made for the same pub. Meyer turned to some men who were watching and one told him, 'Well, what's a chap to do? When he comes out of that 'ere place, there's nowhere else for him to go but the public.'

Meyer promptly rang the bell and asked to see the governor. Miles Walker welcomed him and agreed to co-operate with the idea, which had quickly come to Meyer, that he should invite discharged prisoners to a coffee house which was just three minutes away.

The governor said that, on the first day, Meyer should come inside the prison gates. He admitted that he felt fearful of how the prisoners might treat him and worried how church members might react to his identification with wrong-doers. At 9 am, the gatekeeper let Meyer in and five men were marshalled in a line. Meyer invited them to breakfast at the coffee house as an alternative to the pub. He recalled, 'They all turned and scrutinised me narrowly from head to foot ... one man touched his hat and said, "I'll come, sir, and thankyou kindly."' Then all agreed and, as they walked together, shopkeepers and loiterers stared at them.

Once in the coffee house, its manager, Richard, questioned Meyer as to what he was up to. Meyer explained and he asked, 'Are you doing this on your own head?' On learning he was, Richard replied, 'I would like to give you the first subscription.' The friendship of the manager was an indication to Meyer that God's stamp was on the venture.

Early on, Meyer took a sullen, discharged prisoner to the coffee house. The hot food seemed to thaw him and he told that, on leaving the army, he had got into heavy drinking and finished up a tramp. Meyer commented, 'Something attracted me to this man, who was yet in early manhood, and I felt strongly disposed to help him back to respectability.' Meyer reckoned that in nine cases out of ten, drink had contributed to the crimes which landed the men in prison. He often asked them to sign the pledge and this man complied. He had nowhere to sleep so Meyer took him to a respectable lodging house. He kept off the drink and Meyer found him a job amongst the manufacturers he was getting to know.

His new friend settled in the job and Meyer continued to call. During one visit, the man revealed that he had no living relatives but had once had a girl-friend of whom he spoke fondly. Meyer determined to find her, half-expecting that even if he did so she would be married. By this time, Meyer knew well the poorer parts of Leicester and tracked her down where she was still living with her father. The couple met and began to attend Melbourne Hall and became Christians. After a year, Meyer's heart leapt when asked to marry them. He did so with a policeman as best man. Just before Meyer left Leicester, they began to partake at the Lord's table.

In another example, the discharged prisoner was met by his wife and daughters. Meyer took them to the coffee house where the man promised to sign the pledge if he could have one last pint of porter (ale). Meyer did not want him to go to the pub so went himself where, much to the amazement of the barmaid, he purchased the drink. Back at the coffee house, the man gulped it down, said it was terrible, and proceeded to sign the pledge. Both he and his wife became Christians and, Meyer wrote, were 'transformed and radiant with thankfulness for the blessing which had been brought into their lot.' Meyer added, with some amusement, that the owners of the coffee house complained that he was breaking the rules by bringing in alcohol.

Meyer saw a number of successes. Sometimes he would not see a man for months and then he would drop in the coffee shop, be in employment and return a loan Meyer had made to him. Meyer also acknowledged, ' ... there were many disappointments. Sometimes it would be almost more than I could bear.' The difficulties for discharged prisoners were manifold. One was that many had no homes to return to and accommodation was not easy to find. Some went to what were called common lodging houses which were basic and cheap. The trouble was that their companions there could lure them into trouble. Another difficulty was finding a job for employers were often reluctant to take on men with criminal records.

An unexpected difficulty was that the men might have money. Prisoners could earn 'mark money' by good behaviour. The amount was modest, not more than from £3 to £4, but sufficient to provide immediate shelter and food. Unfortunately, as Meyer witnessed, it could also make for immediate visits to the pub or the gambling den.

Meyer attempted to tackle the 'mark money' through the local Prisoners' Aid Society which he had helped to form and of which he was the honorary agent. The prison authorities agreed, with the prisoners' permission, to entrust the money to the society. After a few weeks, Meyer would return it so that, for instance, a man might purchase a hawker's licence and some stock or the tools required for a new job.

F. B. Meyer, Firewood Merchant

This measure helped just a few. Meyer persuaded some manufacturers to provide jobs but they were not sufficient. He therefore set up his own small project with two men in a cellar chopping wood and making up bundles of firewood. It moved to a two roomed building with more employees while one of the working men from Melbourne Hall brought in his own work as a shoe finisher and also supervised the men. The bundles were sold from a cart and the business just about broke even. All went well in the day. A problem was that, left to their own devices, some of the men ran wild at night.

Then Meyer heard of a yard and workshops, just fifteen minutes from his house, going for a rent of £100 per annum. He realised he would have to act quickly but should he do so? He was on the train to Llandudno 'when as distinctly as possible I became conscious of the impression that I was to go forward; and that my God would be my treasurer and guide.' On his return, Meyer signed an agreement for three years. That evening a friend gave him a donation of £20 which assured him he had made the right decision and he called the place Providence House.

Meyer also had to raise the capital to install a kitchen, a bedroom for nineteen, and a circular saw in the workshop. While this was happening, neighbours began to object, saying that their families would be threatened by criminals and that their house prices would be lowered. These fears were never realised and Meyer thankfully commented, 'In time prejudice was disarmed; and the people would open their windows at our prayer times, that they might hear our men sing the praises of God.' However, there was support as well as opposition. The folk at Melbourne Hall backed their pastor and supplied furnishings and bedding.

Before long the factory was operational with the men earning a modest wage (with deductions for their keep). Living and working on the premises promoted bonds (and a few tensions) between them so that they kept each other out of trouble in the evenings. They produced the firewood which was then sold on two horse-drawn carts with 'F. B. Meyer, Firewood Merchant' painted on the sides.

Just when sales were going well, more serious opposition reared its head. Meyer had become a prominent temperance campaigner and had already provoked anger from publicans who threatened him physically. The publican opposite the prison sent out hostile groups to accost the men who accompanied Meyer to the coffee house. This gradually declined but was followed by opposition from grocers who sold liquor on licence – and Meyer had gone to court to oppose the granting of some licences. The grocers met together and realised they had a weapon to undermine him. They had been amongst the main purchasers of the firewood bundles and now declared they would boycott them. Sales fell by two thirds and piles of unsold bundles began to accumulate.

Meyer looked to 'the chief Partner in the firm' and laid the crisis before Him. Sales began to pick up again. The reason was that customers liked the quality of the Meyer firewood and the grocers realised that they needed it.

Eventually thirty men were living at the accommodation. Meyer would arrive at 7.45 a.m. for prayers and a few hymns. This was followed by discussion and settling of any disputes. A major one arose when some of the men broke the rules by going out for drinks in the evening. Meyer was reluctant to expel them as he cared deeply about them yet he had to uphold the rules. In an inspired moment, he proposed that those who went out drinking would have to leave unless the rest, including Meyer, raised ten shillings for the Prisoners' Aid Society. Soon afterwards, four men went out drinking. Meyer consulted the others and observed how they were interested in their colleagues' welfare. They agreed to contribute the money for them, even though it meant going short themselves. The four were so moved that they stopped drinking. Meyer wrote feelingly that these men 'had noble and generous qualities, crushed by long years of lovelessness, passion, drink, and self-will and waiting for the call of the Saviour.'

The firewood venture proved financially successful. By the time Meyer left Leicester, he had received back all of his own money which he had ploughed into it. But, much more important, it had provided accommodation, work, and a stable life-style for scores of ex-prisoners. In all, it is estimated that Meyer met and helped between 5,000 to 6,000 men at the prison gates. Moreover, he was told that during his time 'the numbers in Leicester Prison had gone down to the extent of there being fifty prisoners less. ... In other words, a large number of the old incorrigibles had been converted and reclaimed, and were no longer turning up time after time for being drunk and disorderly.' As for Providence House, in an eighteen-month period, 140 men passed through it of whom sixty-six obtained work and settled down, three went in the army, thirteen men were still there, thirteen turned out badly, and contact was lost with forty-five. As the study by Kathleen Heasman makes clear, Meyer was not the only Christian minister to take an interest in discharged prisoners. But he was unusual in building a system which offered them both accommodation and work.

In their seminal *British Social Work in the Nineteenth Century*, Young and Ashton are critical of the Discharged Prisoners' Aid Societies which were initiated in the mid-century. They acknowledged that they did give financial aid to some former prisoners but, generally, were not successful in 'helping the ex-prisoner to get on his feet again, and of supporting him in his moments of weakness.' By contrast, Meyer did provide what became called effective after-care, a contribution which is not acknowledged in social work text books.

Prevention
It was put to Meyer that people had to go to prison before he would help them. The statement was unfair but it set him thinking about

starting jobs for men vulnerable to but not yet into crime. He thus bought a ladder and sent out a couple of men to earn their keep by window cleaning. It worked because Meyer's friends hired them. He wanted something that went beyond these friends. He then invested in two of the longest ladders in Leicester, long enough to reach the top windows in large houses, long enough to do factory windows. They were so long that special carts had to be constructed and were pushed by four men. 'Rev. F. B. Meyer's Window-Cleaning Brigade' grew. It gave jobs to unemployed men and, as they cleaned the windows in factories, so they often found better jobs. When they moved on, Meyer could take on new workers.

Still Meyer was not satisfied. He also had compassion for homeless boys and youngsters who had been in prison. He made a part of Providence House into a Home for them. Some were employed in the factory and he found jobs for others in the town. A manager, Mr. William Burnham, was appointed in charge. One day, all the boys ran away and set off for London. Fortunately, the driver of one of the wood carts came across them and soon Mr. Burnham was in pursuit and brought them back. It was then made clear that they were free to leave. None did.

Meyer concluded that to be more like a family, it should be separate from the factory. A house was rented in a neighbouring street where Mr. and Mrs Burnham lovingly cared for the youngsters. After three to four years, the lads were encouraged to move into lodgings. Some kept in touch as they grew to be adults and Meyer was convinced that the Home had prevented some from lives of trouble, unemployment and crime. Years after Meyer moved on, the Home was still flourishing.

More Reaching Out
Meyer's vision seemed unending. He was concerned for the crowds of people who gathered for company, amusement, and often drink in the streets of Leicester. He saw them as sheep without a shepherd. But he could not help them alone. A vital part of Meyer's strategy was to recruit and inspire helpers. He wrote,

'There grew up around me, as with David in the cave of Adullam, not only a nucleus of the younger generation of Leicester's leading families, but a remarkable group of men and women who had been saved by the grace of God, and now loved to save others.' This team was one of Meyer's most successful integrations of middle and working class Christians.

A major problem in the centre of Leicester, as in many parts of Britain, was excessive drinking. Engels explained that working men came home exhausted to overcrowded, poorly furnished homes. The only escape was the cheerful, warm pub where they could drink with their mates and forget work and insecurity. As he put it, 'Liquor is almost the only source of pleasure.' But Engels also perceived that the short-term pleasure led to long-term loss of money and jobs. Whatever the reasons, drinking amongst working class people increased during the nineteenth century. Meyer was campaigning against boozing but wanted something more direct, namely a rescue team to help those who were dangerously drunk in the city.

About 9.30 p.m. on Saturday evenings, the team had supper together and then divided into twos to walk the streets of central Leicester. The markets were still open, the pubs were in full blast. The team stopped fights, took home those who were too drunk to get there, showed kindnesses and spoke words of encouragement. Finding a man from Loughborough in a state of incoherency, Meyer paid his fare, put him on a train and in the charge of the guard. In his pocket he left a note commending him to Christ.

There was one outreach which was conducted just by a small group of ex-prisoners who had given up alcohol and helped Meyer at the prison gates. They asked to do some outreach on their own account in the tramp wards of the workhouse each Sunday afternoon. Having gained permission, they took a service and talked with the tramps who probably listened to them where they might have ignored more wealthy visitors. They then gained entrance to a common lodging house where they impressed the landlord (or keeper). He offered the use of a dirty old loft in the back yard. The men cleaned and repaired it and used it as a meeting place for the neighbourhood. Meyer dubbed it 'the Cathedral'. It attracted people and was still going strong years later.

Another innovation by Meyer – which he was later to use at Christ Church – were outings on Bank holidays. With participants from all sections of the church, he would lead them on walks to neighbouring villages or places of interest in Leicester. Often members of other chapels provided them with tea followed by a short service. Meyer's aim was both to bind the people together in Christian fellowship and to provide recreation for the younger people. At one village, a large cart drew up full of people. To Meyer's delight, it was the congregation from the Cathedral, costermongers, flower-women, hawkers, fruit sellers, some who had been in prison but were now going straight, some who had been drinkers but were now abstainers. His delight was that this was the way they now wanted to spend a Bank holiday.

If one of Meyer's strengths, which he developed in Leicester, was his strategy of recruiting helpers – no one man ministry for him – another was the flowering of his skill in relating with working class people. Meyer had been brought up in a family which, although Christian, kept its distance from those considered socially beneath them. Yet gradually Meyer realised that Jesus was for all people, indeed that he especially loved the poor, the rejected, the foreigner. Over time, he honed the skill and the attitude to step from his middle class upbringing into the lives of the most needy. His training ground was outside the prison gates where he learned how to talk with, not at, discharged prisoners. He was not patronising, persevered with those who rejected him, and won the friendship and loyalty of many. Of course, Meyer could not be one of them in the sense that he always had sufficient money, was never hungry, never in old clothes, never in danger of unemployment. But he did possess an empathy towards them so that he could understand their needs, their anger, their reactions.

Significantly, he seemed happiest with the men and lads at Providence House. Fullerton, recalling the Leicester days, wrote, ' ... he was never so delighted as when he was among the lads, and he proved a real father to some of them.' Later Meyer looked back nostalgically at Christmas time with them. He told of one Christmas day, 'when I was alone, Mrs Meyer being away in France for her health', when five small children knocked at his door at half-past eight in the morning with their Christmas greetings, which they had walked a mile and a half to bring. Then he collected huge amounts of food from the congregation at Melbourne Hall to take to Providence House – 'Puddings to the right of me, puddings to the left of me, puddings in front, on the seat, on the floor of the cab, threatened by floods of gravy.' And finally to a meal with the men and boys who had become his colleagues, indeed his friends.

The reaching out also brought out another unsuspected quality of Meyer to the fore – his courage. As a young man, he was never prominent at physical games. As a pastor, the first impression of him was often of a man retiring in manner and lacking in physical strength. Yet, with the fire of God within him, he stood up at open air meetings in Leicester where he might face verbal abuse. A number of times he was threatened with violence if he appeared in certain streets but he was not put off. Once at Leicester race course, he was recognised as an opponent of gambling. Surrounded by a hostile crowd, he was saved from attack by a shopkeeper, who, despite being a heavy drinker, respected Meyer for his work with ex-prisoners, and somehow got him out.

'Willing to be made willing'

Meyer was such an outstanding social and spiritual figure that it is almost a shock when he admits that in some ways he was very dissatisfied with his Christian life and felt that something was missing. It came to a head in 1884 when he experienced what can be called the second turning point in his ministry.

As a pastor, Meyer had always taken some interest in missionary work. During the second half of the nineteenth century, as A. J. Broomhall makes clear in his massive two volume history *The Shaping of Modern China. Hudson Taylor's Life and Legacy*, British interest intensified. For his part, Meyer invited well-known missionaries to speak at Melbourne Hall. One was Amanda Smith of whom he wrote, 'with her black skin ... singing those slave-songs as only she could sing them, and on her way to evangelise her own people on the West Coast of Africa'. Others were John G. Paton, famed for his exploits in the New Hebrides, and Hudson Taylor, the renowned founder of the China Inland Mission. Then came the Cambridge Seven.

The Cambridge Seven were students (or graduates) of Cambridge University who had volunteered to go to China. They won enormous public interest because of their distinctions and achievements. Charles (usually known by his initials C.T. Studd) was a top England cricketer while Sydney Smith was the stroke for the university's boating crew.

In November 1884, Studd and Smith came to Leicester. They had an immediate effect on Meyer. His support for missionary work never looked back. In addition, there was a more personal impact. He wrote

'The visit of Messrs Stanley Smith and Studd to Melbourne Hall will always mark an epoch in my own life. ... I saw that these young men had something which I had not, but which was within them a constant source of rest and strength and joy.'

The morning after the meeting, Meyer approached them. He continued

Why should I not do what they had done? Why should I not yield my whole nature to God, working out day by day *that* which He would will and work within? Why should I not be a vessel, though only of earthenware, meet for the Master's use, because purged and sanctified?

There was nothing new in what they told me. They said that 'A man must not only believe in Christ for final salvation, but must trust Him for victory over every sin, and for deliverance from every care.' They said, that 'the Lord Jesus was willing to abide in the heart which was wholly yielded up to Him.' They said that 'If there were some things in our lives that made it difficult for us to surrender our whole nature to Christ, yet if we were willing to be made willing to surrender them, He would make us not only willing but glad.'

There was something that Meyer was unwilling to surrender. He went on

I knelt down that night. ... I gave Him an iron ring, the iron ring of my will, with all the keys of my life on it, except one little key that I kept back. And the Master said, 'Are they all here?' I said 'they are all there but one, the key of a tiny closet in my heart, of which I must keep control.' He said, 'If you don't trust Me in all, you don't trust Me at all.' ... He seemed to be receding from me, and I called Him back and said 'I am not willing, but I am willing to be made willing.' It seemed as though He came near and took the key out of my hand, and went straight for the closet. I knew what He would find there, and He knew too. Within a week from that time He had cleared it right out.'

What was the secret closet Meyer wanted to keep? Randall argues, 'it seems probable that it was a sexual temptation.' Fullerton, in a chapter headed 'The Insurgence of Sex' – an unusual title in a book by a Victorian evangelical – makes clear that Meyer later both spoke at meetings of young men and counselled individuals on sexual matters. Randall adds that Meyer rarely spoke 'on matters which were not part of his own experience' which seems to support his sexual interpretation.

Whatever the temptation or problem, Meyer had to yield fully to Christ and there is no doubt he did so. He called it 'Full consecration'. It was a turning point for, before this experience, as he explained, 'My Christian life was spasmodic and fitful; now flaming up with enthusiasm, and then pacing weariedly over leagues of grey ashes and cold cinders.' Thereafter he was more consistent, more stable in his Christian life. In more exciting terms, he said the outcome was 'Fire, fire; Certainty, certainty; Joy, joy.' But still Meyer wanted more.

Background to Keswick

Meyer's consecration experience became public knowledge. This may have been the reason why he was invited to be one of the speakers at the Keswick convention of 1887. Here he was to have his third spiritual turning point, sometimes called his Keswick experience. It was about holiness.

Holiness, the seeking of personal growth in the Christian life, was a major concern to many Christians in the nineteenth century. David Bebbington, in his masterly discussion of this era, identifies four traditions of holiness. Here they can be just outlined and those interested must consult his book *Holiness in Nineteenth-Century England.*

The Anglican High Church tradition which stressed the importance of Christians attending the eucharist (holy communion), worship within a church which contained ceremonies and rituals conducted by robed priests. The similarities to Roman Catholic practice led to the priests being called Anglo-Catholic clergy. Two thirds of them were Oxbridge graduates and Bebbington concluded, 'High church devotion was essentially an elite phenomenon in the nineteenth century.'

The Calvinistic tradition, Bebbington continues, had four characteristics, conversion, a focus on the cross, the Bible as the source of nurture and 'a round of ceaseless activity' in Christian matters. This route to holiness was taught by a number of evangelical Anglicans, Baptists and Congregational ministers.

The Wesleyan tradition, found in various Methodist churches, held the Calvinist characteristics but added that holiness could be advanced by a specific step of faith and that a state of perfect holiness could be attained.

The Keswick tradition was a synthesis of the Calvinist and Wesleyan ones. However, it taught that sin could be repressed but not eradicated. It also placed emphasis on the coming soon of Jesus Christ for the second time.

Meyer had long been a seeker after holiness and, as a young minister, started attending conferences in what was to be the Keswick mould. Some information about them comes from a seventy-six page book of cuttings (mostly written by himself). In July 1874, not long before he left Priory Street Chapel in York, he went to a conference at Broadlands Park, near Romsey, where about a hundred believers waited upon God. A larger meeting was arranged for the following year at Oxford, by which time Meyer had moved to Leicester. He went with his relatives, Mr. and Mrs George Gladstone and the Revd Wade Robinson, whom Meyer had got to know during his teenage years in Brighton. Meyer noted that people of all ranks and churches came together with 'no thought of sect or party, as indeed there never is when the Lord Himself is the centre of unity ... all were present before God, waiting for a second Pentecost.' The main speakers at these gatherings were the Americans, Mr. and Mrs Robert and Hannah Pearsall Smith, who were members of the Society of Friends. Their talks were focussed on the topic of victorious living, with the teaching that holiness was a blessing obtainable by faith rather than something which depended just on the efforts of believers.

There followed other conferences, particularly at London and Brighton, from which emerged the Keswick convention in 1875 which continues until this day. Meyer gives an account of the first Keswick under the leadership of Canon Dundas Hartford Battersby and the Quaker, Robert Wilson. He quotes from material circularised beforehand which spoke of experiencing 'a fuller manifestation of the Holy Spirit's power, whether in subduing the lusts of the flesh, or in enabling them to offer more effective service to God.'

Despite his account, Meyer was not present at the first Keswick, although he began to attend thereafter and it was at Keswick that he had his third major turning point.

Meyer the Romantic?
Before discussing Meyer's personal Keswick experience, it is of interest to divert to ask the question, was he a Romantic? The

Lake District and certain poets who came there were associated with a major movement called Romanticism. Meyer was sometimes described as a spiritual Romantic. Randall says that 'Romanticism and mystical thought helped to shape his (Meyer's) spirituality ... '

David Bebbington explains that Romanticism was a movement which 'emphasised will and emotion ... dwelt on mystery and advocated the natural against the artificial. ...' It originated in eighteenth and nineteenth century literary figures who reacted against industrialisation and materialism. William Blake (1757–1827) wrote poems which bitterly criticised commerce for treating human beings as economic units. Samuel Taylor Coleridge (1772–1834) and William Wordsworth (1770–1850) settled in the Lake District to be near nature. Meyer too perceived the human suffering brought about by commerce. He certainly appreciated the poetry of the Romantics and quoted from them. He did find peace and rest amongst green spaces, his heart was lifted by the sight of its lakes and moved him to write in poetic terms, for instance, 'Immediately beneath and before us, the lake shivers like a silver mirror. Beyond it are the silent hills. Yonder, Skiddaw keeps watch, and far down to the left are the falls of Lodore.'

Meyer wrote that those who lived in great towns 'miss those enlarged conceptions of Nature which are suggested by the far horizon of the sea; the outlines of distant hills ... the outspread panorama of woods, rivers, and pasture lands.' Significantly, he wrote these words in his commentary on the gospel of John where he was discussing God the creator. Unlike some romantic poets, he did not regard nature as a being in itself but rather as an illustration of the goodness of God in creating such beauty.

Further, Meyer also saw the benefits of commerce for mankind. He never lived in a rural area and insisted that God was present in industrial London. He pointed out that nature could not convey the message of the cross.

So Meyer was not a disciple of the Romantic school, which sought ultimate meaning in nature. It should be added that Romanticism was particularly associated with the High Church

Oxford movement with its stress on imagination to be stirred by ceremony and vestments. Meyer would have no part in this.

He was a romantic in the sense that he enjoyed art and beauty as part of God's abundance but not a Romantic who saw them as the pathway to God. His spirituality was partially informed by Romanticism but not formulated by it.

Was he a mystic? Mysticism was a vogue in his day. W. Major Scott in his book on mysticism in 1907 explained that 'vital things are the eternal and unseen things'. Seven years later, in another book, the Revd Wilkinson Riddle defined Christian mysticism as 'the quest of union with God' and certainly Meyer saw himself on that quest. As Randall and Hilborn point out, Meyer sometimes claimed that the unity between different parts of the church was 'mystical' not organisational. But he always argued that Christianity rested on historical events and laws made by God, not simply on emotions and feelings. His later writings may sometimes have dwelt on the mystery and omnipresence of God and on the Christian's close walk with the Master. But this spiritual relationship stemmed from the definite acts of God in the incarnation, the cross, the resurrection and the giving of the Spirit.

The Keswick Experience 1887

Meyer was always keen to advance his own spiritual development, that is his holiness, and in 1887 he had a problem. He was due to address the convention but he did not feel that he had had the Holy Spirit experience of other speakers such as Hudson Taylor. One evening, he walked from the Keswick tent and climbed a hill. He remembered,

> I was too tired to agonise, so I left the prayer meeting and as I walked I said, 'My Father, if there is one soul more than another within the circle of these hills that needs the gift of Pentecost it is I: I want the Holy Spirit but I do not know how to receive Him and I am too weary to think, or feel, or pray intensively.' Then a Voice said to me, 'As you took forgiveness

from the hand of the dying Christ, take the Holy Ghost from the hand of the living Christ, and reckon that the gift is thine by a faith that is utterly indifferent to the presence or absence of resultant joy. According to thy *faith* so shall it be unto thee.' So I turned to Christ and said, 'Lord, as I breathe in this whiff of warm night air, so breathe into every part of me Thy blessed Spirit.' I felt no hand laid on my head, there was no lambent flame, there was no rushing sound from heaven: but by *faith* without emotion, without excitement, I took, and took for the first time, and I have kept on taking ever since.

Meyer did not immediately feel different but his preaching was different. He knew that it had been the Holy Spirit working within him when he first became a Christian by faith. Now he taught that Christians had to receive a deeper filling of the Holy Spirit also by faith, a filling which enabled them to be more holy. He put it thus, 'Christ keeps His faithful servants from falling, moment by moment according to the exercise of faith.' This did not mean, he hastened to add, that they became sinless or perfect but rather that they became more sanctified or holy. Five years later, he wrote in *The Life of Faith* (the Keswick paper) that up to his Keswick experience his inner life had been at a low ebb and that he had been living 'to increase my influence, to make money, to draw audiences and to do philanthropic work.' Meyer, it must be said, was sometimes prone to exaggeration for effect. His statement ignores the fact that during this period he had led many people to Christ and had been a means of strengthening other Christians. It was nonsense, for instance, to suggest that he was out to make money. The difference was that he now relied fully on the power of the Holy Spirit.

His first turning point with Moody widened his horizons to include the masses, changed his concept of the ministry to be less insular and more outward looking, and opened his eyes to the value of other denominations. The second turning point with Studd and Smith enabled him to be rid of a secret sin and so fully consecrated to Christ. The third turning point at Keswick enabled him to claim the continuing power of the Spirit. Moreover, it provided him with the message that the Holy Spirit equipped him and others to live more holy lives. Meyer was not drawn, as far as can be known, into manifestations like speaking in tongues and healings. But he did anticipate that the Holy Spirit would bring revival.

Once accepted on the Keswick platform – and he spoke frequently until his death – Meyer made a number of contributions to the development of the convention. For a start, he taught a practical holiness which countered some of the introversion, even escapism from the world, displayed by some devotees. His experience as a pastor and evangelist enabled him to preach in a way that was relevant to listeners. He showed how holiness had to be expressed in practical actions in everyday life. As Fullerton put it, 'he was less theological and didactic than the others (speakers), more human and sympathetic.' This did not mean he neglected to teach about the Keswick experience for one of his great joys was to lead others into the infilling of the Holy Spirit.

Next, he became the leading Nonconformist Keswick figure. It had been dominated by Anglicans. Meyer's involvement then drew in other Nonconformists under the banner, 'All One in Christ Jesus.' He formed the Baptist Ministers' Prayer Union 'to seek a fuller enduement of the power of the Holy Spirit for themselves and their brethren.' It grew to a membership of over 800. As numbers then attended Keswick or other holiness meetings so they entered more fully into fellowship with ministers from other denominations.

Meyer's growing reputation as a respected evangelical figure also did something to defuse criticisms of Keswick. Herbert Stevenson, editor of *The Life of Faith*, the semi-official voice of Keswick, later wrote, 'In the early days, however, Keswick had to endure considerable misunderstandings and misrepresentation – and not only from non-Christians and those whose antagonism might have been expected; but, strangely, bitter opposition came from fellow Evangelicals. The Convention teaching was denounced as perfectionist, quietist, pentecostalist, and generally unscriptural.' Over time, Meyer dealt with all these criticisms but more his place as a sound teacher of the Bible stood Keswick in good stead.

Not least, he contributed to a greater emphasis on missionary work. Early Keswick leaders had taught that even discussion about missionary work at Keswick distracted the individual from focusing on his personal relationship with God. Meyer and others challenged this and, in the late 1880s, it was agreed to make grants to missionaries in sympathy with Keswick. The first recipient was Amy Carmichael who became well-known for her pioneering missionary work in India and for devotional poetry. Bishop Frank Houghton, in his biography of Amy, reveals that her decision to go abroad must have provoked mixed feelings in Robert Wilson who was in charge of the grants. Following the death of Amy's father, Wilson – a widower – became close to the Carmichael family and especially to Amy, who was the same age as a daughter of Wilson's who had died. Meyer, who sometimes visited Wilson, almost certainly knew Amy as a young person. He participated in her farewell meeting in 1893 in London and in 1899, during his tour of India, he visited her and conducted a mission in her area.

Lastly – and later – he was influential in making Keswick more open to the consideration of social issues.

A final point about Keswick. It accelerated Meyer's writing ministry. In the early 1880s, he had started contributing articles to Christian papers. He also wrote a number of small booklets. *Seven Reasons for Joining the Church* eventually sold 65,000 copies and *Seven Reasons for Believer's Baptism* an astonishing 268,000. Keswick gave him both topics and an audience for larger books. In the ten years following his first message there, he published at least eighteen books. Eight of the books were about the Christian's devotional life and eight were studies of biblical characters, the very topics he spoke on at conventions.

Meyer's theology was now almost complete. He held traditional evangelical beliefs, particularly regarding the divine inspiration of the Bible and the existence of the Trinity. He believed that salvation came by being born again through accepting that Jesus died in our place for our sins – the atonement. As time went by, he increasingly stressed that the coming of Jesus to die stemmed from God's love for humanity. In common with other evangelicals, he held that Christ had risen from the dead, had been taken to heaven and had released His Holy Spirit into the world. He argued that Christians had to consecrate themselves wholly to Christ and then to receive the indwelling power of the Holy Spirit by faith. He took seriously the command to love our neighbours, which he applied by reaching out to serve the needy. In later years, Meyer put more emphasis on the Biblical teaching of the second coming of Christ. But overall Meyer had completed his theology and his conception of the ministry and was ready for the next challenge.

The Leicester Years

Meyer's stay in Leicester had not started promisingly and he cut short his stay at Victoria Road Baptist Chapel. Yet he attracted local support and went on to establish Melbourne Hall where his developing views of the concept of ministry and the role of the church came to fruition.

It had six elements.

First, a core band of evangelical Christians who were regular churchgoers yet not obsessed with one denomination. They were expected to be givers as well as recipients. He developed a system whereby two elders took responsibility for a hundred members and gave them spiritual help where necessary. They also dealt with new applications for church membership. Others, particularly younger members, were expected to participate with him in evangelism and in running the many clubs and agencies associated with the church.

Second, evangelism amongst working-class people, so that the church was a mixture of different sections of the population.

Third, the acceptance of what is called the social gospel, that is, Christians intervening to meet the material and social needs of people in poverty and distress. Of course, the social gospel was not new and its advocates based it on Biblical practice. It experienced a resurgence in Victorian times, part of which was due to the writings of Christian socialists like Frederick Denison Maurice and Charles Kingsley, who were mainly Anglican clergy of liberal theology. It should be explained that they were not socialists in the sense of wanting widespread public ownership (this emerged later). It was rather an appeal for an alleviation of the sufferings of poor people and for an approach which expressed respect for rather than hostility towards the working class. A number of evangelicals were also involved in relieving distress through voluntary agencies. Meyer, however, seemed motivated less by what others said and did and more by what he saw amongst needy people in Leicester. He regarded the social gospel not as an alternative to the spiritual one but as something which went with it, indeed as part of the holistic gospel. As explained, Meyer and his helpers initiated a range of welfare bodies and his social concern was to last for the rest of his life.

Fourth, the centre or hub of the activities was Melbourne Hall. It was open the whole week, not just on Sundays. The traditional gatherings for prayer and Bible study took place there, for Meyer never neglected his responsibility to provide spiritual food for believers. So it did a whole range of educational and recreational activities, with a coffee room opened most evenings. The intention was for it to be a venue where working class men and women would feel comfortable whether they were Christians or not.

Fifth, growing out from the centre was an arm which stretched out to those who could only be contacted on their familiar territory. Meyer and his colleagues went to meet men coming out of prison, got alongside drinkers in the streets and gamblers at the racecourse, spoke to shoppers at the markets.

Sixth, essential provision. Meyer soon perceived that for ex-prisoners, alcoholics and delinquents, conversion was necessary but not always sufficient. Often they also needed jobs and accommodation.

Evangelism and social welfare, a base and outreach, friendship and concrete help: Meyer was not the first minister to shape his ministry on these foundations, but he was an outstanding example. The Leicester years were also notable for Meyer's own spiritual development. The 'willing to be willing' experience with

C.T. Studd and the experience of being filled with the Holy Spirit at Keswick had a profound impact on him. They also opened new horizons and, ironically, may have contributed to his unexpected departure from Leicester.

Leaving Leicester

By the late 1880s, then, Meyer was a successful pastor and a leading figure in Leicester – which is somewhat ironic considering that a deputation had once asked him to leave the city. So why in 1887 did he decide to move away and, indeed, to go to the fashionable Regent's Park Baptist Chapel in London? In some ways he did not want to go and stated, 'I never meant to leave Leicester. I never suffered more than in leaving Leicester. I felt it and so did the people.'

Clearly there were family reasons. Mrs Meyer was always liable to ill-health and the Leicester climate had not proved an improvement on York and Liverpool. Their daughter, who was ten in 1882, had shown early signs of what could have been consumption, although it never developed as such. Significantly, mother and daughter moved to London in 1885. As a husband and father, and particularly as a minister, Meyer did not want to be separated from his family. An article, published in 1907, recorded that during this time, when Meyer was at home on his own, 'he read the words, "So ought husbands to love their wives." It came to him clearly that this was not right. Just at this juncture, Dr. Angus asked whether he would come to Regent's Park Chapel which was then vacant.'

Other reasons were also relevant. After nearly fourteen years non-stop toil, Meyer was tired, if not exhausted. Writing later of the complications of running the factory and Providence House, he said 'I sometimes wonder how I was able to bear the strain of it, combined with my work at the prison, which I never neglected, and my preaching, pastoral, and other ministerial duties.' Noticeably, when discussing his decision to leave, he referred to the downturn in his own health. The folk at Melbourne Hall seemed to appreciate this for, after he received the invitation from Regent's Park, they sent him on a three-week holiday to Algiers.

Despite his exhaustion, he was receiving numerous invitations to speak at campaigns, conventions and conferences. He rarely seemed to refuse. He later wrote of his consecration experience, 'I shall never forget when I first entered into the realisation of the ownership of my Lord: that I was his chattel, and no longer had any option or choice for one's enjoyment or emolument.' He seemed to regard invitations as God-given opportunities to serve the Lord and so not to be declined. These engagements made him well-known. Similarly, Melbourne Hall was the largest Baptist church in Leicester and one of the biggest in Britain. His work with ex-prisoners had been widely reported. A leading article in *The Christian* of 1886 wrote, 'We have seen very much of Church, Sunday-school, and other Christian work on both sides of the Atlantic and on three Continents, but to our mind Melbourne Hall and its pastor stand quite alone.' His emergence as a Keswick speaker also enhanced his reputation, and gave him more writing opportunities and speaking invitations. Keswick may therefore have contributed to his call from the fashionable London church. The demands on his time further exhausted him yet not only did he feel he should accept invitations, he also wanted to have a wider speaking and writing ministry. He could not do this while so busy at Melbourne Hall. He may have felt he could do so at the less demanding Regent's Park.

In addition, Meyer always liked a challenge and, as will be shown, Regent's Park Chapel had its difficulties.

So in early 1888, Meyer accepted the call to London. Leicester citizens wanted to thank him for his services to the city. The mayor, Sir Thomas Wright, presented him with an illuminated address plus the large sum of 400 guineas collected by public subscription.

4

REGENT'S PARK CHAPEL
1888–1892

'A growing influence with the upper classes'

Early in 1888, F. B. Meyer moved to London, which became his home for the rest of his life. It is not clear whether he moved into the accommodation of his wife and daughter or whether they all transported to new and larger premises. The census of 1891 reveals that they lived in Gainsborough Gardens in the suburb of Hampstead, which was close to Hampstead Heath and convenient for Regent's Park.

The fact that Dr. Joseph Angus had acted as an intermediary between Regent's Park Chapel and Meyer is a tribute to the latter. Dr. Angus was principal of Regent's Park College when Meyer studied for the ministry. He was still in that post and would have known many Baptist ministers. Yet he had wanted Meyer, still in his early forties, to lead the prestigious church.

Regent's Park Chapel

Regent's Park was an affluent, residential area near both to the centre of London and to an extensive park and the famous zoo. The chapel, in Park Square East, was set in the middle of a distinguished terrace of houses and had originally been designed to display paintings. Its first minister was Dr. William Landels who, with Dr. William Brock and Charles Spurgeon, made up the great triumvirate of ministers who helped to found the London Baptist Association in 1865.

Landels attracted a wealthy congregation from Regent's Park and further afield. Mann stated that 'the church was a wealthy aristocracy'. His influential ministry closed in 1884, whereupon numbers, financial donations and enthusiasm declined. When the Revd David Davies departed to Hove in 1887, the church leaders recognised their problems and invited Meyer as a pastor who had demonstrated that he could build up a church at Melbourne Hall. Probably it was these very problems which Meyer saw as a challenge. However, he was well aware that Leicester was different from London. At Melbourne Hall, people had been moving into the neighbourhood. At Regent's Park, as in much of central London, there was a move towards the suburbs.

Regent's Park first approached Meyer in October 1887 but Meyer hesitated for weeks. When he did accept at the end of December, he stipulated certain conditions which included that seating in the gallery should be free (given Meyer's views on pew rents it is difficult to understand why he did not apply this to the seating downstairs); the starting of a prayer meeting on Monday evenings; weekly communion; time to pursue his wider ministry, particularly in addressing conferences and conventions; and exemption from routine pastoral visiting – probably this meant that he wanted time to visit non-church members. The church accepted his demands.

Curiously, Meyer's biographers and Meyer himself have little to say about his stay at Regent's Park in contrast to much greater attention to his ministries at Melbourne Hall and Christ Church. Mann gives it half a page; Fullerton has six pages, of which half are about his decision to leave Regent's Park. Jenny Street, who wrote a biography of Meyer up to 1902, simply says 'Mr. Meyer had a growing influence with the upper classes and not a few titled West End residents were among his West End hearers.' Fortunately, Ian Randall's more recent studies have identified some of his achievements there.

Responding to the Challenge

Meyer responded to the challenge and reversed the downward trend. Attendances rose and on Sunday evenings reached 1,500. Writing in the Regent's Park manual for 1890, he stated, 'It is impossible to refrain from reviewing the first two years of my ministry with deep thankfulness.' He frequently urged members to show concern for residents in the immediate neighbourhood, not all of whom were affluent by any means, and particularly to show an interest in the sick and aged. In 1891, he was able to write, 'there is a greater infusion of the social spirit among us but there is always room for growth.' To this end he set up an elected Church Committee, who not only vetted new applications for membership but also visited the needy and decided on the distribution of money from the church's poor fund.

In terms of numbers, in 1888, 126 people were added to the church membership, of whom fifty-nine were by transfer from other churches and sixty-seven by profession of faith. This trend continued throughout Meyer's time there

Financial giving also improved. In 1892 Meyer recorded, 'the renovation of our Sanctuary was most successfully carried out, and it often seems to me, as I see it in the evening, radiant with the electric light, and filled with people, as beautiful a Sanctuary as I could desire.'

The work with children also grew and not only on Sundays. During the winter months, a class for children was held on Saturdays along with a number of groups during the week.

Reasons for his Success

What explains Meyer's success? He would have attributed it to prayer and, certainly, the introduction of the Monday evening prayer meeting, at which he encouraged women to participate, did raise the spiritual temperature of the church. There can be no doubt that Meyer's reputation as, and ability as, a preacher drew in some from other churches and some who had stopped attending. In his zest for evangelism, Meyer door-knocked in the immediate vicinity and probably drew in some local people.

In 1891, his friend Fullerton, who had a growing reputation as an evangelist, led a successful mission at Regent's Park. These outreaches must have contributed to the high proportion of new members who joined following conversion.

Not least, Meyer seemed to have learned from his disputes at Priory Street Chapel and Victoria Road Chapel. He had no disagreements with the elders (there were no deacons at Regent's Park) who included some very prominent citizens. He had a friendly and welcoming approach towards church members and on Saturday afternoons he opened his home to any who wanted to enjoy food, talk and relaxation. He possessed, or developed, a non-pulpit style on social occasions and was a cheerful, often humorous, host.

Meyer was never content with the *status quo*. He had a nose for spotting new needs, to see people whom the church was not serving. He initiated a Thursday service for business people, the forerunner of the lunchtime services which some churches today hold in busy city centres. Meyer had worked in a junior capacity as an office worker and would have known that many young men moved to London for similar positions but were often lonely in their digs. So on Sunday afternoons he inaugurated a young men's class which was followed by tea. They could then remain in the building for the rest of the day to read the literature or just to enjoy each other's company.

A little known theme of Meyer's ministries was his recognition of the spiritual abilities of women. With rare exceptions, British churches used women as tea making, flower arranging and sale of work fodder – although many went to the mission field. Other denominations had recruited women as deaconesses and Meyer and others in the London Baptist Association founded the Baptist Deaconesses Home and Mission in 1890. Historian John Briggs stated, 'He was the genius behind the birth of the Baptist deaconesses order, which equipped and trained women to give leadership to the churches to engage with the social problems, particularly the absence of medical care, in the inner city.'

The successful pastor of a fashionable London church, a regular contributor to the Christian press and a popular author, it is not surprising that Meyer became well-known in Christian circles. He was regularly invited to speak at missions which, a report in *The Quiver* magazine noted 'are on the subject of Christian living'. Somehow he managed to fit in a twice a week commitment at the East London Missionary Training Institute (Harley College) in Bow. It was run by Grattan Guinness, described as 'a gentleman evangelist' who had played a major part in the Ulster revival of 1859. He was a friend of Hudson Taylor and Dr. Barnardo, and an enthusiast for missionary work. His college trained 1,330 missionaries for forty missionary societies. He and Meyer held each other in mutual respect.

There followed Meyer's first speaking engagements abroad. In 1891 he went to the USA at Moody's invitation to speak at his well-established Northfield conference. More will be said about Meyer's travels in a later chapter. Mann, in his biography, says much about Meyer in America and here it is sufficient to draw upon a few of his observations for 1891. Meyer spoke twice daily for two weeks. Mann records the judgment of one commentator, 'Of all the great teachers and preachers whom Mr. Moody has brought from afar to his annual Conferences at Northfield, no one has more thoroughly won all hearts than F. B. Meyer.' Such was his impact that Moody persuaded him to give extra Bible readings for a week after the conference was supposed to have closed. He then took him to speak to students and others at his Bible Institute in Chicago. Meyer was promptly invited back for 1892 and this time he went accompanied by his wife.

Some Disappointments

Regent's Park Chapel had long been a church for the well-to-do. Perhaps Meyer hoped to change that as part of the challenge. If so he was probably disappointed. He did establish an Institute for Working Lads, a meeting for older youngsters in the neighbourhood. But he did not draw in working class people on the scale he had at Melbourne Hall. The chapel had not completely neglected 'the lower orders' and supported a Domestic Mission in one of the poorer areas in Camden Town, which had its own Sunday services, Workmen's Club, Mutual Aid Society, and Penny Bank (which had nearly 1,400 depositors in the year *before* Meyer arrived). Meyer makes no mention of this work. The reason was almost certainly that he did not want to keep the poor at arms' length. Indeed, he later wrote in 1899, 'There has been too great a tendency in the present day to relegate work among the poor to Mission Halls, instead of encouraging all classes to meet at least on one day in the week, beneath a common roof.' His vision was of placing outreach and welfare services within the main church. He wanted to break down class differences between Christians, not reinforce them.

He did find an outlet for his social mission within the London Baptist Association, which had launched the Forward Movement in 1889 to promote the social work of its chapels. Meyer became its honorary superintendent and the historian, Kathleen Heasman, says that he showed particular skill in bringing together the various shades of belief and action within the Baptist denomination. One project established a lodging house to take men off the streets in Holborn. One of the elders at Regent's Park, Dr. Percy Lush, gave his medical services to it.

Meyer became president of the London Baptist Association. Presidents usually marked their time in office by some achievement and Meyer wanted to build a chapel in a deprived part of the East End of London. This never happened but it showed where his heart was.

At Melbourne Hall, despite some limitations, Meyer did reach people in the bottom rungs of society. In so doing, with all his other commitments, he exhausted himself to the extent that he had to leave. At Regent's Park, he did not carry such a load but he felt dissatisfied, even guilty, that he was not reaching the masses in the immediate neighbourhood. It was no consolation working one-removed from the front line through the Forward Movement. No doubt this drawback contributed to his next bombshell.

In 1892, Meyer did it again. He suddenly resigned from Regents Park and announced that he was to become pastor at Christ Church, Westminster.

Leaving Regent's Park

After thirty-eight years of service, the minister or pastor of Christ Church in south London, Newman Hall, was to retire in 1892. The idea of inviting Meyer seems to have originated with him. An entry in his diary for that year read, 'It was reported that the Rev. F. B. Meyer, pastor of Regent's Park Baptist Church, was being urged by Mr. Moody to join him in evangelistic work in America. Let us also approach him to evangelise in South London as president of all our operations, known as he is, and honoured for godliness, eloquence, usefulness, and evangelistic zeal.' Noticeably, Newman Hall had been one of the speakers at the opening of Melbourne Hall.

Nothing more is known about Moody's urgings or Meyer's response. It is known that Christ Church began to negotiate with Meyer in what was described by Randall as 'great secrecy'. Amongst the negotiators were, almost certainly, Newman Hall himself and George Williams, a trustee at Christ Church and a leading evangelical who had played a large part in founding the YMCA and who would be known by Meyer. On June 18th, a meeting of the trustees and elders of Christ Church agreed that Meyer should be nominated to succeed Newman Hall. On June 27th, a meeting of church members approved the nomination. On July 16th, Meyer wrote to Christ Church to arrange a meeting with the trustees and elders and did so five days later. At the end of July, he informed a shocked Regent's Park Chapel that he had accepted the invitation to Christ Church.

Newman Hall was delighted. He attended Keswick that year where Meyer was speaking. His hand-written letter to Christ Church is still preserved. He wrote, 'The most impressive and instructive of all (the speakers) I have heard is your new Pastor and my dear Friend ... his style of preaching must be admired for its dignity, purity and deep impressiveness. Calm – thoughtful

– but often rising to the highest eloquence, listened to by all with rapt attention but what is far better revealing such knowledge of Scripture – such searching of heart. ... I felt after hearing him that I wished I had to begin my fifty years again – for I would by God's help be a better preacher and pastor than I had been.'

Not so delighted were the members of Regent's Park Chapel. In its Church Year Book following Meyer's departure, it said that 1892 had opened with high hopes and more people joining the church until rumours suggested that Meyer was about to leave. It continued that the announcement that he was departing for another church 'was received with regret and dismay'. The report graciously thanked Meyer for the numbers of people he had brought to know Jesus Christ in the past four years and for the agencies he had set up in the neighbourhood. However, there was no doubt that officials and members at Regent's Park felt badly treated by the suddenness and manner of his going.

It is difficult to understand why Meyer did not immediately inform Regent's Park that he had been approached by Christ Church. They would then have been fully aware of the possibility of his departure. Fullerton, who knew Meyer better than most, suggested that Meyer was sure that God was calling him to Christ Church but 'he dared not risk the pressure that would have been surely brought to bear on him had he consulted the Church, or even conferred with its officers'. Fullerton adds that this was not the only time Meyer acted in this fashion. It might be thought that a strong character like Meyer, if convinced of the call, could have withstood any pressure. However, as will be shown, years later he was persuaded to stay on at Christ Church after saying he was about to leave. Meyer clearly felt guilty about his sudden withdrawal and wrote a long letter of explanation to Regent's Park which he had printed and circulated. He expressed regret at causing pain to members by his departure. He added that the 'meagre congregation' and 'the lessened stipend, indicate that I am not animated by mercenary motives in contemplating the exchange.' Meyer's stipend at Christ Church was £300, which was much less than he had received at the smaller Victoria

Road Chapel in Leicester. Perhaps the decline in attendances and activities at Christ Church constituted another challenge for Meyer. He then gave three further reasons for his decision. The first was 'a conviction ... that our Lord and Master, the chief Shepherd of the flock, is calling me thither.'

The second was 'I was never an ardent denominationalist.' This may seem strange in that Meyer had allowed himself to be appointed president of the London Baptist Association and had participated in Baptist Union matters. However, Meyer indicated that he found it restrictive to be bound to one denomination and wanted to be 'equally in touch with all sections of the Evangelical Christians'.

He added that he did not wish to take 'an active part in a controversy for which I have neither inclination nor adaption'. This is probably a reference to a long drawn out internal dispute within the Baptist Union which started in 1887 when Spurgeon, and others who shared his views, resigned on the grounds that some Baptist ministers no longer held traditional conservative evangelical beliefs. Meyer spent much time and effort acting as a reconciler. Later, Meyer was involved in another controversy when the minister at Pembroke Chapel exchanged pulpits with a Unitarian minister who apparently denied the deity of Christ. Meyer declared that it should not have happened but refused to regard it as a reason for leaving the Baptist Union – for which he was criticised by some evangelicals. He did not want to devote so much time to denominational controversies. This did not mean that Meyer ceased to believe in the practice of baptism. Indeed, one of his conditions for accepting the position at Christ Church – which had only loose denominational connections – was that a baptistry be built in the church.

The third reason was Meyer's desire to serve the poor. The role of the church towards poor people was being discussed in Nonconformist circles. In 1883, the London Congregational Union had published *The Bitter Cry of Outcast London* by Andrew Mearns which criticised the widening gap between churches and 'the lowest classes'. Meyer might well have considered that he had been more in touch with them in Leicester than at Regent's Park. He wrote, 'I have often questioned whether I was acting consistently with my deepest principles, to be officiating as the minister of an influential and successful church, drawing a large salary, and surrounded by every sign of success, and welcomed in all parts of the country as a popular preacher, whilst the great masses of the people were living in sin and need in the more densely-populated districts of London.' There is no doubt that Meyer missed the involvement with working class people which he had pioneered in Leicester. It is also worth adding that William Booth published his *In Darkest England and the Way Out* in 1890. To my knowledge Meyer does not write about it but he knew Booth and the book caused such an uproar that he must have known of it and of its call to Christians to be alongside the poor. Certainly, Christ Church, with its neighbourhood of Lambeth, was in one of the most deprived areas of London. Moving to Christ Church would open the door to the masses. Jenny Street wrote that he accepted the invitation to Christ Church 'because he believed it was possible to carry out in Lambeth the work he had begun at Leicester'. His acceptance of the challenge at Christ Church did not mean he meant to cut down on his wider ministry. Even before he went to the church, he was on the boat to the USA.

5

CHRIST CHURCH: THE HEIGHT OF HIS MINISTRY
1892–1907

'The blending of high and low'

The origins of Christ Church go back to the remarkable Rowland Hill, who was born to a wealthy family at Hawkstone Hall, Shropshire, in 1744. A fervent evangelist, he had difficulty in obtaining ordination and, even when he did, was not acceptable in many pulpits. With a large inheritance from his father, he built Surrey Chapel in what is now Blackfriars Road in London. Its octagonal shape was, apparently, chosen by Hill so that the devil would have no corners to hide in. Opened in 1783, it was never allied to any denomination and its evangelical preaching drew large crowds. The first ragged school in London was started and other Sunday Schools came under the auspices of the Southwark Sunday School Society. Also established were a Benevolent Society and almshouses for elderly people.

Hill died in 1833, to be succeeded by the Revd James Sherman whom Meyer could remember visiting the home of his parents. Sherman doubled the membership and then, in 1854, was succeeded by Dr. Newman Hall. The son of a heavy drinking father, who later became a Christian, Newman Hall became a strong advocate of temperance as well as a visionary minister. The lease on Surrey Chapel was due to expire in 1883 and he looked for a new site in the vicinity. Eventually, the congregation purchased a freehold at Asylum Cross (an asylum for female orphans had once stood there) at the junction between Kennington Road and Westminster Bridge Road. Newman Hall influenced the design of the new church and the large gothic Christ Church and Hawkstone Hall were opened for worship in 1876. It was still not officially attached to any main denomination. Newman Hall was well-known in the USA and had been a strong supporter of the North in the American Civil War. Americans contributed towards the building of the Lincoln Tower, next to Christ Church, also opened in that year.

The congregation had left Surrey Chapel a few years before the lease ended and it was handed over to the Primitive Methodists. Subsequently they moved on to build another Surrey Chapel also in Blackfriars Road. Their pastor was the Revd Benjamin Senior who wrote up its story in a book published in 1892. The old Surrey Chapel was not pulled down but was converted – if that is right word – into a famous boxing hall, 'the ring'.

'A Forlorn Hope'

Meyer's ministry at Christ Church commenced at the end of September 1892. As well as his condition about the installation of a baptistry, he had also insisted on having Tuesdays and Wednesdays free for his ministry outside of Christ Church, that gallery seats should be free, that communion be held every Sunday and that all church meetings would be chaired by himself. He agreed, with regret, to the church's stipulation that he wore his B.A. gown in the pulpit.

The church had wanted Meyer to live within walking distance of the church. No doubt, he would have welcomed this but he could not impose it upon his wife. Eventually, he installed a bedroom and study within the church and lived there at weekends. Mrs Meyer was never the conventional minister's wife who ran the women's meetings. It appears that she was not a regular attender on Sundays. Census records show that their daughter married in 1893 in Hampstead to Edward Charles Tatam, of whom little if anything is known. The Christ Church Magazine of 1894 announced that the Tatams had a son on August 19th at Brighton (they eventually had two daughters as well). Meyer was in the USA at the time and the magazine congratulated him on becoming a grandfather. Strangely, no mention was made of his wife.

Unlike many ministers in large churches, Meyer did not initially have an assistant pastor but he was granted the services of a full-time male secretary. The man appointed was H. G. Turner, who had had extensive administrative experience with Lambeth Borough Council. A committed Christian, Turner proved to be more than a secretary and became fully involved in the life of the church. By 1894, Meyer also obtained an assistant minister, the Revd W. J. Wintle. He did not enjoy good health and took on editing the Christ Church Magazine which Meyer had introduced. Soon after, he took charge of the small South London Missionary Training Institute which Meyer had founded, particularly for recruits from Christ Church. In 1898, Wintle was replaced by the Revd A. W. Evans.

Meyer's first sermon appears to have been preached on the last Sunday in September. *The Christian Commonwealth* reported it very fully. His text was taken from 2 Corinthians, chapter 4, verse 2, 'By manifestation of the truth commending ourselves to every man's conscience in the sight of God' (KJV). His theme was the Christian ministry and he made two main points. One was that the minister's aim was to touch people's consciences. He said, 'And I hope as God shall lead me in this place as the days go on that I shall grapple with the conscience which is in the heart of every man and which shall be compelled to respond to the manifestation of the truth of God.' The other was that his weapon was the truth as 'ensphered in the Gospel of Jesus Christ'. He continued that in presenting the truth he had two allies, the power of the Holy Ghost and the consciences of every heart in the audience who would respond to Him.

Meyer concluded that if the response of his listeners was to say that his message was 'a fine sermon' and no more then he had failed. He would be a success only 'if a conscience was moved and a penitent cried "God have mercy on me a sinner"'.

Sermons on a Sunday were one thing, starting on the following Monday was another. Meyer faced a daunting task. Jennie Street wrote that Meyer's acceptance of the post at Christ Church 'looked to some like undertaking a forlorn hope and there were some confident prophecies that his heroic venture would end in failure and disappointment. It was not merely that Christ Church had steadily declined in prosperity as the neighbourhood around it deteriorated: the costly cathedral-like edifice with its shadowy aisles, lofty roof and imperfect acoustics was – and is – very unsuitable for mission purposes.'

The words of the journalist, Street, were confirmed by a minister in the patch. The Revd Tolfree Parr was pastor of the New Surrey Chapel not far from Christ Church. He wrote,

> The conditions of the people around our Central London Churches is entirely adverse to spiritual success. The high pressure of life; the conditions of labour, with its long hours, uncertainty, low pay, and horrible monotony; the ceaseless struggle with poverty – 50 to 60 per cent of the population around some of our chapels living below the poverty line; the crowded and unhealthy dwellings; the sordid and degrading pleasures; the curse of drink, entire populations almost besotted with it; the vice and immorality of some districts transforming them into veritable Gomorrahs; the secular spirit destroying the holy quiet of the Sabbath; the widespread and utter religious apathy – these are some of the conditions of life around us.

He continued that many middle class residents had moved to the suburbs, leaving the churches bereft of worshippers, workers and money.

In addition, the neighbourhood around Christ Church was notorious for brothels and drinking houses. In 1854, a select committee of the House of Lords identified the New Cut (a road close to the church) as having sixteen public houses which were usually full of drinkers, including women and children.

If Meyer relished a challenge then Christ Church was his most daunting one.

Building Church Membership

Meyer's initial priority was to re-build the church's membership and attendance, which had dropped to about one hundred on Sunday evenings. He wanted to restore existing members whose attendance had declined. London always contained Christians who had just moved to the capital and others who were dissatisfied with their present churches, and Meyer was aware that his preaching could draw them to Christ Church. Above all, he desired additions from new converts.

But there was a more mercenary but no less Christian motive. Christ Church was not sound financially. The huge building was expensive to maintain and Meyer wanted more money to fund the new initiatives he had in mind. More people on Sundays meant more money in the collections. Sometimes, he made special appeals. In Easter 1894 he wrote a letter to members and friends explaining that essential repairs to the heating apparatus would cost £60, mending the roof £30, a further ladies' lavatory and repairs in Hawkstone Hall another £50, and the Sunday School Society was in debt to the extent of £130. In all he asked for £300 and, apparently, it was forthcoming.

The Christ Church Archives for the period from September 1892 to June 1894 contain just over a hundred letters from and to Meyer. These included letters of thanks, with one woman thanking him for his personal care during a bereavement. Another had drifted away but had been helped by Meyer's booklet *The First Steps to a Blessed Life* and wanted to see him. There were letters requesting personal financial support, for instance, one from a sixty-three year old lady, who had joined Surrey Chapel in 1863, and whose husband had not worked for seven years because of chronic bronchitis and heart disease. One was a request from a widow with four children, asking if Meyer could get one of them into an orphanage. Another letter from a mother thanked him for getting her daughter into an 'Orphan School'.

The bulk of the correspondence was about church membership. These could be formal notes from churches, commending their former members who were transferring to Christ Church or a smaller number indicating that former Christ Church members were now in their fold. They reveal that a number of members from Regent's Park followed Meyer to Christ Church. Following the death of the foremost Baptist leader, Charles Haddon Spurgeon, in 1892, there were some disagreements within the Metropolitan Tabernacle and a number of members transferred to Christ Church.

Other letters were hand-written requests to join. One letter, dated 26 September 1892, came from a Mr. Walter Bacon, who lived in Waterloo Road, and must have warmed Meyer's heart. He told how in 1887 Meyer's booklet *Seven Rules for Daily Living* had helped him and he had 'asked the Lord to make me willing to be willing to yield my business to God'. A year later he lost the business but 'I consciously received through the exercise of faith, the gift of the Holy Ghost.' While Meyer was at Regent's Park, Mr. Bacon searched for a house near that chapel for himself, wife and eight children but the rents were too high. He was delighted when Meyer moved to Christ Church 'and I should like to have my name and that of my wife entered upon your church roll'.

Randall calculates that in four years the church membership escalated to about 1,000. The fact that between 1892 and 1907 about 1,500 people were baptised indicates that many were new believers rather than transferred from other churches. Following a census of London churches in 1902 to 1903, the Revd Mudie-Smith stated that Christ Church had the highest attendance of any church in Lambeth and gave a figure of 2,046, which combined attendances at both a morning and evening service. Randall says that attendances at evening services rose to 2,300. These figures are not incompatible as they were probably recorded in different years. Randall justly concludes that 'Christ Church became once more one of London's most prominent Nonconformist churches.'

Strengthening Christians
Meyer was always convinced that the Sunday diet was not sufficient to feed Christian growth. He soon introduced the Monday prayer meeting. On Thursdays he held a service and

sermon at 12 noon (this may have been for office staff in the vicinity). On Friday evening, he conducted a Bible reading. He also wanted something for younger Christians. In 1893, he launched the Young Men's Christian Union with seventy attending its monthly consecration meeting. Topics for talks and discussion included, 'Loyalty to Jesus Christ', 'Self-Denial', 'Purity' and, inevitably, 'Total Abstinence'. A little later came the Young Women's Christian Union. The Pleasant Thursday Evening (P.T.E.) started in 1892. The big difference was that the P.T.E. was for both young men and women, with an emphasis on social enjoyment. It started late so as to suit those employed in shops. Meyer nearly always led it with a bright talk on something like 'Ideal husbands and wives' for he was keen that young Christians should marry partners who were also in the faith. By 1894, it was drawing in between 300 to 400 young people.

Within the P.T.E., Meyer set up a book fund to last for twenty-one weeks. A leaflet explaining its rules remains in the archives. Participants paid in a penny a week and if they completed eighteen payments could choose a book – apparently selected by the organisers. In addition, they would receive an autographed book by Meyer valued at 2/6d.

The movement was still flourishing after six years when Meyer gave a talk on great people, including the former Liberal leader, William Gladstone. Meyer remained a staunch Liberal.

The Brotherhood

Meyer wrote in the Christ Church Magazine, 'Glad as I am to welcome friends from all parts who come to our services, I feel that our true mission is not to cater for these but to meet the need of the dense masses of people that live within daily sight of our glorious and beautiful temple.' Trouble was, as Fullerton pointed out, the temple 'seemed overwhelmingly grand to those who lived in tenements, and almost repellent to the abject poor'.

But Meyer came with the experience of his years in Leicester. He went to the tenements. He visited the neighbourhood and soon became a familiar and acceptable figure. A contemporary journalist wrote of the poorer local residents, 'Their humble homes were invaded, not by a supercilious, condescending person from another walk in life, but by a warm-hearted understanding individual.' He decided to adopt the approach of the Pleasant Sunday Afternoon movement. It had started in 1874 under the Revd John Blackham in West Bromwich who adopted Moody style tactics – a short snappy talk, music, participation from the audience – to draw working men. It spread rapidly to 1,700 branches in Britain. A criticism of some branches was that any Christian content was outweighed by the amusements. Meyer was convinced the two could be combined.

Fourteen men, along with the tireless H. G. Turner, volunteered to help. They took out invitations and it started in the church on a Sunday afternoon in December 1893. The appointed singer failed to turn up and men came in, but slowly, and looked lost in the vast church. Then more entered, making two hundred in all, and they actually applauded the speakers. Meyer seemed uneasy with the name Pleasant Sunday Afternoon and suggested that they call each others 'brothers'. His suggestion was also greeted with clapping and the meeting became known as the Brotherhood or the P.S.A. Brotherhood. Meyer was its president and Turner the secretary.

There followed a Supper Party. After a meal of meat – Meyer pointed out that working men, unlike usual church goers, did not care much for cakes – trays of tobacco were handed around. Meyer did not like smoking but, he wrote, 'It has always been a habit of mine in these things to let God's Spirit dictate what a man shall do and shall not do. We have no right to add to the Ten Commandments in the earlier stages of the Christian Life.' At this occasion. Meyer was full of banter and humour. The men took to him.

The Sunday meetings took off. Social issues were raised. For instance, it was agreed to petition the council to start wash-houses in the neighbourhood. Then came a fifteen minute talk, usually by Meyer. Fullerton observed that he seemed to have 'almost a dual personality'. On Sunday mornings and evenings, he was the dignified and eloquent ecclesiastic while in the afternoons he was 'bluff and cheerful ... challenging the best in the men'. But it was no soft gospel. Meyer preached both the need to find salvation through Christ and the need to give up alcohol. Indeed, one corner of the church was Consecration Corner, for those desiring to become Christians, and one Teetotal Corner, for those wishing to sign the pledge.

Fullerton occasionally gave the address and at one his theme was that men needed to change boats and serve a better skipper, Jesus. Some of the men observed that Meyer was their skipper in Lambeth and henceforth referred to him by that title – which he loved.

As time went by, organisations grew up within the Brotherhood. One was the visiting committee in which the men themselves visited members who had not been for a few weeks or who were sick. It was a work they carried out in the evenings, after long hours at work. But there were encouragements. A visitor reported the contents of one of his visits in the Christ Church Magazine. The husband had rejoiced. 'I have been pouring twelve shillings a week down my throat but, thank God, since I came to the PSA and signed the pledge, things are growing different here now.' His wife added, 'Yes, for now we have been able to buy half a dozen chairs, that table, and a looking glass, with the money that used to go to drink.' The historian, Frank Prochaska, points out that visiting was one of the more important forms of charitable activity in Victorian Britain. But usually it was the middle classes, particularly women, visiting their social inferiors. By contrast, the Brotherhood visiting entailed working men calling on people of their own class.

At other times, they went on 'public house raids', usually about closing time on Saturday nights and would bring back from forty to fifty drunken people, give them strong coffee accompanied by music from the Brotherhood's own brass band and then tell them about Jesus.

Teams of members would sometimes take services in other places. In 1895, they conducted Sunday evening services in the small King's Court Mission in nearby Great Suffolk Street. A number decided to participate regularly and by 1898 it was drawing in much larger congregations and had a meeting for children with 130 attending.

Under Turner's leadership, free education classes started on subjects like writing, shorthand, arithmetic, chemistry, history and singing. They could lead to examinations and were inspected by official government inspectors. They proved popular, took on the name of the P.S.A Adult School, and expanded into another building, the Institute in Kennington Road. Important classes added later were for those unable to read or write, and book-keeping. By 1898, the School had been visited three times by inspectors who were 'well pleased'. Turner played a big part in the Brotherhood and it was appropriate that in 1898, 1,500 men and women gathered to present Mr. and Mrs Turner with a silver tea and coffee set to mark their twenty-fifth wedding anniversary.

In an era when state unemployment benefits did not exist, unemployment due to illness was a constant anxiety. The Brotherhood organised a Benefit Society in which members could contribute small amounts each week and receive help for short periods when out of work. They could also save money with the Brotherhood to be drawn out later for clothes or a daughter's wedding. Meyer commented, 'It is enough to bring tears to one's eyes, to think of many of our men taking their wives and children for a week at Margate, which would have been an impossibility in the old drinking days.' The Brotherhood, again probably through Turner, made links with employers and jobs were found for a number of members.

Other Brotherhood groups were smaller (possibly more temporary) but important. On Saturday nights there was a temperance meeting, apparently for those needing the support of each other at a time when they were most likely to go to the pub. Meyer sometimes said that P.S.A. stood for Perfect Salvation Always. Another group used to come together on Sunday mornings – it must have been before the main service – for a deeper spiritual gathering. Whatever the need of the men, temporary or long-term, Meyer and Turner tried to address it.

The Brotherhood grew steadily. In May 1894, it had a member-ship of five to six hundred and an attendance of eight hundred at the main Sunday meetings, with over a thousand on special occasions. A year later it was reported that, since the start, 360 men had signed the pledge not to drink. A journalist who attended one of the meetings in 1900 reported, 'It was an audience to inspire any preacher. There were a few elderly men and a sprinkling of young lads, but the vast majority were men in the full vigour of life, most of them between twenty and forty years of age. From the opening hymn to the benediction at the close the attention and interest never flagged. The cheery sympathy of Mr. Meyer who presided, had evidently established a thoroughly good understanding between himself and his audience.'

In 1905 Meyer, as part of the Brotherhood, founded the Nelson Coffee House in Lower Marsh, Lambeth. Perhaps the idea sprang from his memories of happy times in coffee houses in Leicester. The Nelson sold food as well as coffee. Meyer boasted 'Our beef-steak puddings challenge the world.' It had a number of purposes. One was an attractive alternative to the nearby pubs. Another was the provision of cheap food in one of London's poorest districts. It was also a place where women could attend as well as men (in contrast to pubs, where men often left their wives at home). At lunch-times, working girls could get a hot meal for two pence. Upstairs were beds at six pence a night and it also included a club room for the Brotherhood. It proved an instant attraction and drew the crowds.

In July 1899, the great social scientist, Charles Booth, interviewed H. G. Turner for his study of London churches. His handwritten report – sometimes hard to decipher – is lodged in the archives of the London School of Economics. Booth stated. 'My talk with Mr. Turner turned chiefly round the P.S.A. Brotherhood which has been his main work for the church.' He drew upon Turner's words to show the rapid growth of the movement and added, 'Though Mr. Meyer originally enthused Mr. Turner, he is now I think the moving spirit of the P.S.A. He evidently lives for it: in order to take up this work he gave up a position where his salary was double what it is now, "but," he said, "the last few years have been the happiest years of my life."'

Booth rightly assessed that Turner was one reason why the Brotherhood was so successful. What were the other reasons? Clearly it met a need in a district where the pubs had dominated. Meyer and Turner's tactic of involving men as participants not just as recipients must have played a part. Clearly the men felt respected and, in exchange, they respected the leaders. Probably most important was Meyer's ability – unusual in a person from his background – to relate with working men. He not only respected, he also liked, even loved them. He never played down the vices which were displayed in the lives of some working class people, for he had close acquaintance with them. But he was able to put these evils in the context of the appalling circumstances in which many lived. He developed an empathy with them so that he could almost put himself in their shoes. For instance, Meyer was a Sabbatarian, that is he wanted Sundays to be kept as God's day with no trade or commerce. Yet he realised that many poor people had to buy food on a Sunday. He explained, 'I know under what miserable conditions our poor people are compelled to live, and I for one would not ask them to keep their vegetables and meat for a number of hours in the stifling atmosphere of their overcrowded homes. You must first improve the condition of the people before you can do away altogether with Sunday trading.' He appreciated their strengths and potential. Looking around at the crowds in the Nelson and those who served them, he said, 'Who will despair of Old England, as long as the working men and their wives are as true and as loyal as ours? God bless them! Talk about the Smart Set, they are not to be mentioned in the same breath.' A bit over the top, but justified.

Not least, Meyer could communicate with his audience. A number of visitors to the Brotherhood commented on this. His biographer, Chester Mann, was one. He wrote, 'He was at his best in his relation to his Men's Brotherhood. ... What *a way* the man had with him, to be sure! Neither before, nor since, have I seen or heard a man who, with such consummate ease, commanded the attention and compelled the interest of working men to the consideration of moral issues.'

In 1895, Meyer had a holiday in Switzerland where he did some mountain climbing. When he returned, the Brotherhood arranged a welcome at their first Sunday meeting at which wives and children were invited, making an audience of up to 1,400. When Meyer entered, the crowd broke into 'Praise God from whom all blessings flow' and clapping. He was then presented with a book in which were testimonies from fifty men who had been blessed by him. When Meyer responded, he was overcome with emotion. But soon he was himself, delivering a message and evoking laughter as he described his efforts on ice on his holiday.

After another trip to the USA a similar book was presented. One letter was from a man who joined the Brotherhood two years before. He had worked in twenty-two taverns and been discharged from all, except one, for drunkenness. He wrote, 'I am pleased to tell you that I am a pledge Abstainer ever since I joined the P.S.A., and thank God, He has enabled me to keep it. ... I have now regained my lost character.'

Another favourite example of Meyer's he called 'The dead canary'. The theme at the Brotherhood meeting had been 'For Jesus' sake'. One man returned to his flat where his favourite canary was dead and his wife in fear of a beating. When she told him, he responded, 'Well, it can't be helped, it's alright for His sake.' When Meyer heard, he sent him the best canary money could buy with the simple note 'For Jesus' sake'.

The affection in which Meyer was held by at least some working men is revealed in another oft-repeated story. Meyer was being loudly heckled by one man at a temperance meeting. A burly workman turned round and said quietly but firmly, 'Shut up, you fool. That's Meyer, as good a man as ever stepped in shoe leather. You don't know that man, or you'd soon dry up.' He did dry up.

Women's At Home

The success of the Brotherhood led to requests for something similar for women. Meyer had also noticed the difficulties for some men who had signed the pledge but whose wives were heavy drinkers. He stated, 'It is not at all an infrequent case for a man to break out in prayer for his wife, and if there is heroism anywhere it is surely evidenced in the new convert who, as he returns home day after day from his work, needing his tea and rest, is never sure whether his first act may not have to be to seek for his wife dead drunk in an untidy room, or drinking in some neighbourly public house.'

The result was The Women's At Home (sometimes called The Mothers' At Home) in Hawkstone Hall on Monday afternoons, run initially by female volunteers from the church. One hundred and fifty women came to the first meeting, where they found they did not sit in rows but around tables with a pot of tea. A creche was provided for small children. A Help Fund was started for anyone in difficulties. Soon the attendance rose to two hundred and fifty. The format and style was similar to that for the Brotherhood, with a light approach combined with a Christian message, and some emphasis on giving up heavy drinking. Meyer nearly always led the meetings, would ask wives who had kissed their husbands good morning to raise their hands and get a laugh when he wondered why one woman raised both hands. The talks by outside speakers were often about health, cooking, abstinence, followed by tea and biscuits, with the piano in the background. Meyer understood the hard, tiring and poverty-stricken lives led by many of the women and one of his great joys was to see their faces light up with a smile. In December 1898, just before he was due to leave for India, the Christ Church Magazine made note of a meeting at which the Revd A. Evans sang and played the cornet. Meyer was there for the whole time and revelled in the occasion. The magazine stated, 'However tired or depressed we may have been feeling, Mr. Meyer has something to make us laugh and know that all the brightness has not gone away from life.'

Reaching Out

The Brotherhood, and the Women's At Home, were the result of Meyer and his helpers reaching out into the homes of residents in the surrounding district and drawing them into Christ Church. A more direct form of reaching out in order to win men for Christ concerned regular visits to lodging houses of the kind Meyer had first encountered in Leicester. The occupants of these institutions did not have homes of their own. Meyer appeared content to leave this work in the hands of a group of Christ Church men who, on most Sundays, visited four lodging houses. They had friendly chats with the occupants and usually conducted a brief service for those who were interested. Every now and then, they invited the men back to Christ Church for a meal. Conversions did take place. One man who had 'by scoff and insult done all he could to annoy the workers – was led to trust the Lord Jesus and has since added to his profession of faith, the irrefutable testimony of a changed life'. A moving story concerned the proprietress of one of the lodging houses, who was robbed of all her money while ill in bed and so faced eviction. A man, who had been converted in that very place and had gone on to make good, intervened to replace her loss.

This work proved a good training ground for some of the visitors. In a four-month period in 1898, five went on 'direct service' with three training for the mission field and two for the home ministry.

It did not need organised action to reach out. Meyer walked the neighbourhood, was adept at chatting with people in the street, and was blessed with the gift of repartee with cabmen and cart drivers. After a laugh with Meyer, one driver said to his mates, 'He'll wash', that is, 'He's alright.'

Meeting Need

In a district of poverty, Meyer was determined to meet some material needs. He did not start from scratch. A Benevolent Society which was 109 years old, and had apparently been taken over by Surrey Chapel, still existed. It distributed small amounts of financial help and blankets. Meyer placed it under the charge of a number of Christ Church members, who wrote about it in the church magazine of 1894. They gave examples of people who had been helped: a middle aged man, with a family, prostrated with blindness; an elderly and lame woman with no family; a woman with a daughter suffering from skin disease and a husband, after twenty-five years in a job, thrown out to make way for a younger man. Some of those helped did join the Brotherhood or Women's at Home, or the children started at the Sunday School.

More substantial were the almshouses which had been founded at Surrey Chapel. The best known was the Rowland Hill Almshouses which contained twenty-three elderly women. Its huge minutes book is still in existence in the Christ Church Archives. The lease had expired in 1870 and the trustees continued to rent the site. The houses were in poor condition but a Mrs Atley had left a considerable amount to erect a new building. Meyer's arrival – he took over as chairman – coincided with discussions whether to build on a nearby site, which would avoid having to move the residents from their familiar neighbourhood or to a more healthy area in the country. The latter view prevailed and, on 27 June 1895, Meyer opened a modern building with more extensive grounds in Ashford, Kent.

Meyer was also concerned about the needs of young, working girls. He may well have been influenced by Dwight Moody, who had noticed the lack of evening facilities for factory and other working girls. In Lambeth, the girls often hung around the streets in the evenings or outside pubs and were vulnerable to sexual advances or being drawn into crime. What to do? Meyer told the story of how he took thirty to forty girls on a Bank Holiday outing to Barnes. As soon as they arrived, an organ-grinder started playing a polka and soon they were dancing with male 'cousins' who had mysteriously appeared. He concluded. 'We all went home together in some third class carriages – I, more dead than alive.'

This appears to have been the start in 1893 of the Girls' Evening Home (sometimes called the Working Girls' Home) which was opened in Oakley Street in the neighbourhood. It was led by Sister Elsie, who lived on the premises. It is not clear who owned the house or who employed her but Meyer was clearly the moving spirit.

Sister Elsie had hit upon the idea of an evening girl's club, with the atmosphere of a home, for teenage working girls. Its aim was that 'of providing a bright, cheery place where the poor and hard-working girls of the neighbourhood could find rest, recreation, sympathy and help'. It soon became popular, with about forty girls crowding in each evening. In late 1893, the Christ Church Magazine reported that Sister Elsie had brought thirty girls to their first Sale of Work in Hawkstone Hall. It said of the girls, 'and all belonged to that very rough class which we had in view when the Home was first contemplated'. Hopefully the girls did not read this description of themselves. They enjoyed a magic lantern show and a lady phrenologist. It raised £150.

A further report a year later said that the girls participated in educational classes, singing, and cookery. The girls had been wild at first, but under Sister Elsie's gentle yet firm approach had settled down. She did not press religion on them but numbers accompanied her to church and later some did become church members. Meyer seemed a frequent and popular visitor and joined in a New Year's treat in 1894, with a supper of roast beef and plum pudding followed by a bran pie, out of which every girl drew a warm winter garment. A few months later, the girls led a sing-song at a packed Hawkstone Hall, after which Sister Elsie made a plea for situations, that is jobs, for the girls. In 1890, she took sixteen of the girls on holiday to Portishead. Young and Ashton record that at this time little provision was made for girls outside their homes. The work of Sister Elsie, backed by Meyer, was therefore in the vanguard of social action.

What of lads, as Meyer called them? He saw numbers as he walked in the neighbourhood. He had doubts whether the wild and rough ones would enter a club attached to a church. He invited them to coffee and buns at the Lambeth Baths in 1895 where, at a noisy gathering, he outlined his plans for a club and some were enthusiastic. At the close, two of the volunteer helpers found that their coats had disappeared. 'Ah, well' said Meyer, 'We have evidently got a hold of the right sort at last.'

He wanted to start a Working Lads' Institute and, after some false starts, obtained an old factory in the last stages of dilapidation. Volunteers restored it and soon it had a refreshment bar with cheap, hot food, games room, a gym, rooms for education, and a stable for band practice. Membership was limited to fifty and gradually behaviour improved. In 1898, they gave a gymnastic display, attended by many from Christ Church. A glowing Meyer presided and a report stated, 'This work among the roughest lads is very dear to the pastor's heart.' A story, repeated in a number of sources, is that Meyer's team worked closely with a family called Hooligan, from which the word 'hooligan' passed into the language. Later, the Institute took in younger boys who became part of the Boys' Brigade movement.

January and February of 1895 were marked by extreme cold and continual frosts which caused much suffering amongst those with little money and in damp, unheated accommodation. Meyer quickly formed a team. They had few resources and no time to raise money but the dominating feeling was 'These people must be relieved, and God will provide the wherewithal.' They sought out and delivered food and coal to the most distressed. A wholesome dinner was provided for over two hundred children as often as possible. In one home of an unemployed man, his heavily pregnant wife was lying on a straw mattress with nothing to cover her but a threadbare quilt. They had no food until the team found them. The girls from the Evening Home also played their part. They quickly made quilts and took them and soup to nearby families. Meyer insisted that the aim was not evangelism but relief to those in desperate need.

Some of the women in the church went out in the evenings to talk with the 'unhappy sisters found on the main streets'. A number went back to the church for warmth and food. Perhaps the church premises were not acceptable for, a few months later, they were operating from Jurston Hall on Thursday evenings for 'young women who wander the streets'. In addition, Meyer financially supported Sister Margaret Graham who opened her home each night for prostitutes. She told of one prostitute who heard Meyer preach and said, 'Ain't he lovely: he wouldn't condemn you.' On another Sunday evening, she took three women to Christ Church. Meyer did not know of their presence but preached, 'God can make spoiled lives good: let Him make yours good.' Two of the women immediately renounced prostitution while the third did so eventually. Sister Margaret provoked hostility from men, presumably pimps, and suffered physical violence at times. But she would not retreat and was active until her death at the age of seventy-one in 1938. Meyer sometimes spoke about the need for the gospel to be 'incarnated again'. Sisters Margaret and Elsie were outstanding examples of Christians who were incarnated at the hard end of society.

There were other ventures of which the records make brief and insufficient mention. Meyer devised a Needlework Fund in which women donated old garments to the church which were then distributed to others in the immediate neighbourhood who were good with the needle and used the materials for new clothes. The church then purchased them back. Very soon 660 garments had been completed, which meant that the needle women had earned some money in their own homes while the church had clothes to give to those in need or to sell at its annual Sale of Work. In 1894, the church purchased 37 Clapham Road as accommodation at moderate rents for twelve young business men. Mr. Turner kept a watchful eye on it.

Meyer was not the only minister and not the only social activist in Lambeth. It is worth mentioning that Octavia Hill, one of the founders of modern social work, was working in the 1880s in Lambeth in improving and managing property for poor tenants. This was a branch of meeting social need which Meyer did not pursue. Octavia came in and undertook her work at the request of the Ecclessiatical Commissioners. Meyer's contribution was outstanding in that his presence in the area enabled him to identify and quickly respond to situations which were causing social distress to people he knew.

Recreation

Meyer was keen on the church premises being used for recreational purposes. It made the building more a part of the neighbourhood where people, perhaps with no interest in religion, would make use of its facilities. Further, it was an alternative to some more dubious amusements – by which Meyer meant pubs and the music hall.

He launched the Hawkstone Hall Institute (or Young Men's Institute) in 1890 for young men aged fourteen and over and it soon attracted large numbers. Again, much of the responsibility fell on the willing shoulders of H. G. Turner. Meyer was often away on Tuesdays and Wednesdays on speaking engagements and, increasingly, on tours abroad. It was Turner who provided the continuity.

The activities included football and cricket teams, tennis (in which women also participated), a gym, swimming, cycling (usually Saturday runs but also cycling races), educational classes, an annual camp and a reading room and library. All for three shillings and sixpence a year.

Its educational classes appeared to compete for space with those of the Brotherhood, which later transferred to another building. Amongst them were 'Ambulance Lectures', given by Dr. Oswald, a member of the church, and which led to a St. John's Ambulance Association certificate. The camp entailed about twenty young men sleeping in farm buildings near the sea. They engaged in swimming, sport, walks, cooking for themselves.

The football and cricket teams, usually two of each, were taken seriously with reports written up in the magazine. Meyer found a decent football pitch and Hawkstone Hall F.C. proved one of the best teams in south London. In 1894, some members were keen to join a league. This sparked a debate. One letter in the magazine noted that league players were often paid and, as a result, the writer noticed 'how frequently fouls are given, players are cautioned, the offside rule is broken, and, alas, penalty kicks also occur'. The team remained amateur. A report made in December of that year noted that the team was undefeated having won five, drawn three, with one abandoned due to the weather. The writer complained that in one of the draws, the equaliser came near the end when 'we had only the light of the moon to guide us and a goal was given against us which we feel went outside the post. We of course had to submit to his (the referee's) decision.'

These were the days before goal nets and showing dissent. The team was looking forward to a game with the Crown Court F.C. whose team was 'entirely composed of Scotchmen so the match may appropriately be termed England v Scotland'. In 1895, five hundred young men and women gathered in Hawkstone Hall to celebrate the Institute's anniversary. After food, songs and lantern slides, and an exhibition of music drill with dumb bells, Meyer gave out the prizes for tennis, cricket, football and cycling.

Noticing that Saturday evening was the time when families most wanted recreation, Meyer opened Hawkstone Hall at 8 p.m. to husbands, wives and children. Meyer always tried to be there 'because I want to show them that a Christian may be bright and happy, without descending to the vulgar or stupid'. He added that it also gave him the chance to get to know those families who were usually out when he called in the week. After a hymn, there was a sing-song of traditional songs and recitations, followed by refreshments and chat. Meyer would then give not a sermon but a comment on something he had seen in the papers or an experience from his travels. Often people were urged to take the pledge. As people left, often slowly, some of his helpers would be preparing the hall for Sunday School.

Another activity which Meyer continued from his Leicester days was an outing on Bank holidays. At Easter 1894, he accompanied two hundred to Egham in glorious sunny weather, which finished with food and 'a bright gospel service' in the Wesleyan Chapel. At Whitsun, they went to Barnes. On Boxing Day 1895, the energetic Meyer and ten others walked from Waterloo to Wimbledon while a larger number went by train. They then all walked across the Common, had lunch at Surbiton and then back to Wimbledon. Here they were joined by seventy more and walked again to a Congregational Church for tea. Meyer asked anyone to tell the party which Biblical texts they had found helpful in their Christian lives. On Easter Monday 1898, Turner did the organising and, apparently, the walking. Meyer went by train – he was over fifty by this date. In all, 360 sat down to tea at Richmond, followed by two open air meetings and an evening meeting at Duke Street Chapel, which Meyer had helped to start while a student.

These outings were largely for church members and those who attended Hawkstone Hall. Christ Church also had The Poor People's Annual Excursion. The name may sound patronising today but, in July 1895, seven hundred crowded into a train to Herne Bay. Having organised many day outings myself (never more than a hundred), I wonder how they never lost anybody.

Children

Most of the numerous activities outlined in this section have been for adults or teenagers. Children were not overlooked. On Sundays, the demand was such that children's services were held in Hawkstone Hall at 9.30 and 11 a.m. and 2.45 and 6.30 p.m. Frank Prochaska, in his recent study, points out that attendances at Sunday Schools started to decline from the 1880s. Not so at Christ Church, where the reverse happened.

As with the adults, leisure activities were not ignored. A Children's Recreation Club met after school one evening a week for two hours. Children crowded in to play skittles, draughts, tug-of-war and to learn drill. The latter kept them warm as sometimes supplies for the heater ran low. Holidays were arranged annually. In 1894, for instance, a re-union was held for fifty boys, who had been to Poltescoe the previous August, with Meyer there as usual. For the Sunday School holiday, it was noted that many had to be paid for, as parents could not afford the money. In addition, twenty boys from the Sunday School, probably the more boisterous ones, were taken for four days to East Grinstead. Their high spirits prevented them having much sleep on the first night and, on the following day, football, cricket and an eight mile walk must have tired them out.

Mention must be made of the Southwark Sunday Schools Society which Christ Church had inherited from Surrey Chapel. It consisted of eleven Sunday Schools which drew in hundreds of children. The organisation was demanding in terms of time and personnel but Meyer took it on enthusiastically. He chaired the annual meeting in 1895, where the report explained that the work also included the Band of Hope, Christian Endeavour, Parents' Meetings, Christmas treats and holidays. In all, the number of children coming under the umbrella of Christ Church must have numbered many hundreds.

Christian Endeavour – a movement for nurturing and training fifty-seven Christian young people – was close to Meyer's heart. He started a Christ Church branch soon after he arrived and put it in the hands of a talented and dedicated woman, with Meyer attending once a month. The emphasis was on getting young Christians, up to the age of seventeen, to serve others, by tract distribution, holding meetings for small children, and having Sunday evening gatherings (in the lads' factory) for some of the poorest children in the area. Meyer took a close interest and, in 1894, became the first president of the Central South London Christian Endeavour Union. A report of the Christ Church branch in 1894 noted that it had its own lending library and that a sick member had been sent to St. Leonard's for a fortnight. In 1899, Meyer was elected its national president and travelled extensively to visit branches and meetings and to extend its membership. The same year, he published a short book called *I Promise*, made up of six pithy chapters to encourage young believers.

Political Trend

Meyer once wrote, 'God does not deal with society as a whole, but with individuals one by one ... not with politics but with principles.' He never altered his belief in the importance of evangelism to ensure that people were brought into an individual relationship with God. He then moved on to argue that the combined efforts of these individuals could set an example which might influence society as a whole.

At Leicester and even more at Christ Church, for instance, Meyer remained a strong supporter of the temperance movement, which aimed to help individuals break free from strong drink. He was an enthusiastic supporter of the Blue Ribbon movement, in which supporters publicly wore a ribbon to show they were abstainers. He frequently spoke at temperance meetings and opened Christ Church to their gatherings. In early 1897, the Christ Church branch of the British Women's Temperance Association held a tea for a hundred men and women 'who were known to be far from abstemious'. Twenty-six signed the pledge cards. A few weeks after the meeting, it was noted that a Christian woman saw the answers to her prayers when her husband, a heavy drinker for twenty-seven years, had kept from strong drink for four weeks, had obtained work and was attending the Brotherhood.

A year later, the British Women's Temperance Association held its half-yearly meeting at Christ Church with up to three hundred present. The attraction was Miss Hallie Q. Smith, 'the Afro-American orator, singer and reciter'. Twenty signed the pledge and at the end a number of people crowded on the platform to shake hands and show their appreciation of Miss Smith.

All this was essential in that it changed individuals. In his book *Reveries and Realities*, Meyer provided stirring examples of individuals who did turn permanently from drink and also acknowledged some failures. But it was not sufficient. Meyer moved on to collective action whereby pressure was put on local authorities to apply the laws which controlled the sale of liquor and on government to make them more stringent. He was incensed that grocers could obtain licences to sell alcohol and passionately asked 'when will the working men have the right to secure immunity for their wives and families by prohibiting the sale of drink along their streets?' As in Leicester, Meyer joined other ministers in opposing the granting and renewal of some licences. He considered magistrates, 'in their luxurious mansions', who dealt with licensing, to be completely out of touch with the havoc caused by drink. He then campaigned for laws to give local authorities greater powers to control the numbers of pubs. He urged the government to be more pro-active in tackling the menace of drink.

In May 1895, he presided over a public meeting in Hawkstone Hall to support the Intoxicating Liquor Traffic (Local Control) Bill to give greater power to local electors to prohibit the sale of liquor. The meeting may seem unremarkable but numbers of evangelical churches were opposed to their buildings being used for political purposes. On a different subject, they would not have approved a debate in Christ Church that narrowly passed the motion 'That women should have equal electoral rights with men'. Oddly enough, the organising body was a forum of young men and no women seemed to participate. Meyer became marked as a minister prepared to influence government.

Meyer took a great interest in sexual purity. In central London, his lectures to young men – which drew audiences of up to a thousand – on the right and wrong use of sex were, Fullerton records, 'brutally intimate'. But his major concern was for misused and misled young women. He noted the limitations of rescue work amongst prostitutes and vulnerable young people which hauled a few out of the swamp but did not drain it. Brothels were illegal but any action depended upon complaints from two ratepayers. The local councils of Lambeth, Southwark and Bermondsey, tended to avoid their responsibilities. Meyer, working through the Central South London Free Church Council, collected facts about the numbers using brothels and put pressure on the authorities to prosecute. He worked closely with police and local councillors while he and his colleagues were prepared to give evidence in court of what they had seen. Meyer's able assistant Turner told how they watched one house for five hours one evening and saw one woman take twenty-three men into it. The result was that up to eight hundred brothels were closed in his years at Christ Church, although Meyer and his team had to face hostility and threats from brothel owners and users.

Meyer also moved in his analysis of poverty. In London, and probably before, he held that poverty was not just the result of individual fecklessness but was linked with the appalling conditions in which millions were made to live. He developed this to throw some responsibility on to the rich and wrote,

The foreigner is amazed at Hyde Park in the height of the season; such equipages, liveries, dresses, jewels, display. He doesn't visit the East End, to see that the wealth of London is very unequal in its distribution, and that the few are rich, because uncounted thousands are compelled to exist in the most destitute and miserable poverty.

He certainly called upon the wealthy to use their money to help the poor and he was approaching the point of arguing for the state to intervene on their behalf – an unusual position for a conservative evangelical. His changing view on the role of the state was in keeping with the time. The historian Arthur Bryant explains that the Reform Act of 1867 extended the vote to more male artisans who 'leant not towards the classic liberalism of *laissez-faire* but towards ... social reform' and called upon government to act to modify the adverse effects of capitalism. Their views were incorporated by the growing numbers within trade unions.

Meyer's political views were also shaped by his experience within the Brotherhood. In 1905, he wrote a remarkable article in *The Quiver* entitled 'My P.S.A. Brothers'. He was an astute observer of political and social developments and he dwelt on the increasing acting together of working men. He wrote, 'Probably never before in English history have such vast congregations of working men gathered systematically on Sunday afternoons. The keynote of these gatherings is Brotherhood; their basis and constitution are absolutely democratic; and where the true ideal is realised, the character, teachings, and work of Jesus Christ are the one attractive and all-satisfying theme.' He continued, 'Men are ceasing to believe that the individual is the true unit of society, and that the law of social progress is to be found in rivalry and competition. They are becoming conscious of the possibility of a common life and destiny. They are coming to feel that they are members one of another, and that the weakest cannot languish without detriment to the whole.' Clearly, Meyer was referring to the growing socialist movement, with its emphasis on co-operation and collectivity. Chris Bryant MP and Graham Dale point out that a number of early socialists were also Christians. Indeed before Meyer left Christ Church some had been elected as Labour MPs. One was Will Crooks, who rose from being a child in the workhouse to MP for Woolwich. I have a copy of his biography in which, as the inscription in the front shows, was presented by the Hawick P.S.A. Brotherhood in 1910 to one, G. Wallace. Another was Arthur Henderson, who, soon after being elected an MP in 1903, was in lodgings in Kennington Road close to Christ Church, although he would have worshipped at the nearest Wesleyan Methodist church. His biographer says that he spoke at temperance and Brotherhood meetings 'in which he took a keen interest'. Henderson later became a cabinet minister and leader of the Labour party.

Turner called Meyer 'practically a Christian socialist'. During this period he showed a great sympathy towards socialism and the Labour party because he saw links between the teachings of Jesus and some socialist practices. He also encouraged Christians to become involved in politics. In one of his popular books of daily readings, *Our Daily Walk*, Meyer commended the Good Samaritan for tending the robbed and injured man. He added that action was needed to make the road safe at all times. He continued, 'Perhaps the better policy is to get ourselves elected on the Council or Magistrates' bench, so that we may put down the gangs of thieves which infest life's highways.' Importantly, he was stressing that inner holiness was not at odds with outward political action. Meyer frequently urged Christians to stand in municipal elections. Without actually saying which political party people should vote for, he issued manifestoes 'to direct our people in the exercise of their civic and political rights'. Turner was elected a Poor Law Guardian in Lambeth while Meyer himself was elected a councillor of the borough, although little is known of his activities on the council.

Since a young man, Meyer had been interested in politics but it was at Leicester and, even more, at Christ Church that his interests developed into action. His biographer, Chester Mann, concluded, 'He became a Christian politician.' He was now at the point of calling for state intervention to relieve social problems such as poverty. He was not alone in so doing but, it must be added, there was strong opposition. Most business figures feared that any growth in state involvement would harm the free market. The secretary of the influential Charity Organisation Society, Charles Loch, was a Christian who argued publicly that individuals were responsible for their own poverty and that state help would weaken their resolve. But was Meyer a socialist? The answer will be in the next chapter.

'The blending of high and low'

In 1899 Meyer stated, 'Our church stands for the blending of high and low beneath one roof.' He added that it was his belief 'that the division between the classes of our country must not be allowed to increase, and that if any bridge between them is to be discovered it must be through the ministry of the church.' He regarded such mixing as an integral part of the Christian life. In his study of the book of Romans, *The Dedicated Life*, he imagines a middle class member of the church walking in the street and coming across '*a man of low estate*' (his italics) who also goes to the church. He writes, 'The pavement is full of fashionably-dressed folk with whom you are anxious to stand well. ... These people would surely misinterpret you if you were to be seen in conversation with some humble member of your Church. But you refuse to entertain the suggestion. You remember that what is highly esteemed among men is abomination in the sight of God; ... you associate freely with one of your humbler brethren to your great enrichment and to his comfort.'

That Meyer had to write such words reflects the rigid class distinctions within Victorian society. They rarely mixed in terms of friendship. Meyer considered this as unchristian and wanted a church, like that of the New Testament, where people of all ranks were in comfortable fellowship in Christ. Did he succeed? Did he integrate the Victorian classes at Christ Church?

His evangelism resulted in many conversions. Towards the end of his life he claimed that in almost every seat in Christ Church (and it held 2,500 people) someone had sat who had become a Christian. Many of these were working class people converted within the Brotherhood and the Women's at Home movements. As previously mentioned, during his ministry at Christ Church about 1,500 people were baptised as believers.

What of those who joined the church? Records show that numbers were professional or business people, including doctors and an MP. Others were working people. A handwritten note by Meyer (probably from 1893) lists eight candidates for membership. They were all local people, and included a 'gas purifier, converted 3-4 months ago', the 'wife of a caretaker', 'a tailor, brought by his brother' and 'a young person, newly converted'. All were accepted for membership but Meyer thought that a young woman 'Converted last Monday' should wait. On 14 April 1894, Meyer noted that an eighty-one year old woman had the call to become a member, 'a very poor woman, after having paid her rent she has only 1s left'. On 6th May 1894, up to thirty members of the Brotherhood joined the church and the magazine recorded that Meyer 'was visibly affected by the scene – the first fruits of many months anxious work and prayer'. By 1898, church membership had increased to 1,009. Of recent joiners, the magazine noted 'most admitted from the world', that is not by transfer from other churches.

Turner's comments, as reported by Charles Booth, are instructive. He wrote that Turner emphasised Meyer's aim 'to break down the class barrier and he brought numbers of the poor of the neighbourhood to the church. A third of the congregation, Mr. Turner thinks, would be working class.' Turner added that not only did working class people attend but they were on friendly terms with those from the middle classes.

All the indications are that considerable numbers of working class people did join Christ Church and did attend on Sunday mornings or evenings – in addition to the overwhelmingly working class attendance at the Brotherhood on Sunday afternoons. But Meyer was probably not wholly satisfied. The evening service was still conducted on the liturgical lines inherited from Surrey Chapel and beloved by older and more traditional members. Meyer had accepted this as a condition when he came to Christ Church.

None the less, he wanted to adopt, not a bright Brotherhood-style service, but one in which the congregation felt more involved, that is the worship came from their hearts, not from a set service which could be regarded as oldfashioned. The church elders were divided and Meyer did not push it.

None the less, writing in 1907, Meyer rejoiced in the changing social structure within Christ Church. He wrote,

> The older people connected with the Church have in many cases passed away, many families have gone to reside in the suburbs, the ebb of the population has been inevitable and unceasing but we have shown that it is possible to make a great Gothic Church the home of the people of the neighbourhood. Though but few carriages drive up to its doors the men and women who live around look up to the soaring spire of the Church, and feel that it marks their home, the one spot on earth where they have received love, welcome, hope and inspiration. Not now the Church of the classes, the noble building has become the home of the masses. ... We have shown that it is possible for a congregation which contains no wealthy men or endowment to raise yearly an income of between five and six thousand pounds.

Meyer can be forgiven for, as he sometimes did in his writings, going over the top. He gives the impression that Christ Church had almost lost its middle class members. In fact, in a study written about the London church census of 1902 to 1903, Charles Masterman concluded that, although Lambeth was the poorest district in South London, it still drew in some of 'the well-to-do' from other areas. Some of these continued as elders, as helpers and as those who still wanted the traditional evening service.

But Meyer did have considerable success both in winning working class people to Christ and drawing them alongside more affluent believers within the church. During this period there were evangelical churches which drew in large middle class congregations and concentrated on their needs. There were those, like Spurgeon's Metropolitan Tabernacle, which drew in a similar congregation yet also ran social welfare activities and a mission hall outwith the main church. By contrast, the Salvation Army, although it did not call itself a church, had 'soldiers' and followers who, at least in its early decades, were mainly from working class backgrounds. Christ Church was unusual in the extent to which it did integrate different sections of society. This achievement was the more remarkable in that Meyer started with a small congregation of middle class members, a lack of funds and without the financial backers he had enjoyed at the start of his work at Melbourne Hall.

Height of his Ministry

In later life, Meyer looked back on Leicester as his great years, the days he would like to relive. His nostalgia is understandable, it was at Melbourne Hall that he made his breakthrough into combining evangelism with social welfare and where, every day, he was personally involved at the prison gates. Yet, my assessment is that his first ministry at Christ Church was the height of his ministry. For these reasons.

First, the numbers of conversions, baptisms, those joining the church (especially from working class backgrounds), those signing the pledge, were more numerous at Christ Church than at Melbourne Hall, even taking into account his longer time scale at Christ Church. Perhaps more important, integration of different classes occurred at Christ Church.

Second, the P.S.A. Brotherhood was a large, local organisation which had no counterpart in Leicester. It is worth recording that, in a study published in 1904, the Revd E. Goold stated that the Brotherhood was not as successful in London as in other parts of the country because 'the chasm between him (the working man) and the churches is deeper and broader.' He continued that there were two exceptions. The largest Brotherhoods were in Ilford in outer London (which my grandfather attended) and Christ Church.

Third, Meyer was able to give more attention to the needs of women at Christ Church, particularly through the Women's At Home and through the efforts of Sisters Elsie and Margaret.

Fourth, it was at Christ Church that Meyer established a large number of recreational activities which served the whole community.

Fifth, the range of social welfare activity was remarkable. In London, Meyer did not repeat the outstanding work he did with ex-prisoners and did not provide jobs for them. On the other hand, he did promote the club for working girls. He oversaw help and accommodation for prostitutes. He took over, improved and extended the almshouses for elderly women. He determined to help the most demanding working lads and set up an institute for them. The police paid tribute to Meyer's efforts; an inspector said that there were fewer in the police cells because of him, and sometimes called on him to take a young delinquent in hand. Not least, Meyer mobilised the church to take seriously its responsibilities towards those in social distress.

Sixth, much more than at Leicester, Meyer challenged public authorities to tackle the problems of drink and sexual abuse. His work for social purity became recognised beyond the Nonconformist churches and later drew praise from the Archbishop of Canterbury, Randall Davidson.

Seventh, Meyer recruited helpers, even more than in his previous pastorates. Indeed, the scale of the work would have been impossible without them. Sisters Elsie and Margaret, Mr. Turner and assistant ministers worked full-time. It is not clear who employed the sisters, although Meyer seems to have supplied at least part of their financial support. In addition, Meyer expected church members, if at all possible, to be involved in running activities. The Sunday Schools and youth activities required an army of helpers to organise and teach. In the magazine, one Sunday School teacher told how he took his duties seriously. He always wrote to the boys in his charge on their birthdays as a boy 'so rarely receives a letter from anyone that when he does get one, he generally treasures it'. With two other teachers, he took the boys for cricket on Saturday afternoons and on outings.

Meyer ensured that his volunteers included working people. Sometimes he needed to convince them about their latent powers but, given the opportunities and confidence, 'they have stepped up to the level of which they were capable.' When he finally left Christ Church in 1907, Meyer numbered the volunteers in their 'Thousands' and called them 'many of the noblest men and women I have ever known'. He particularly mentioned the Visiting Committee of the Brotherhood who for fifteen years had gone out 'night after night to visit the sick and dying in the neighbourhood'.

Eighth, he was immensely popular with the membership. After a trip to India and Burma with his wife in 1898 to 1899, the church packed Hawkstone Hall to welcome them back. Meyer replied that he had seen many wonderful sights abroad but, on return three things were even more wonderful, the sight of the chalk cliff of England, the spire of Christ Church and 'your faces'. He was greeted with cheer after cheer. He was not just popular but loved. And he loved Christ Church. In his mid seventies, when people asked for his address, he still said, 'Christ Church, London, – till I die'.

If Meyer's ministry was at its height in Christ Church, this is not to decry the importance of the Leicester experience. It was there that he established the model of his ministry, namely a core of evangelical members who were not fixated with denomination; evangelism amongst the working class; a mixture of both the social and spiritual gospels; the church as the hub of activities for church members and local citizens; an arm of action which went to the territory of people who would not enter the church; and the provision of essentials like accommodation and jobs for the homeless.

He stuck to this model at Christ Church, although on a larger scale and with outreach to, and provision for, different groups of needy people. The hub, namely the huge gothic church and Hawkstone Hall, was larger than Melbourne Hall but was soon filled to overflowing. Consequently, as with Providence House, there were outposts like the Working Lads Institute, the homes of Sisters Margaret and Elsie, a hostel for office workers, the Nelson Coffee House and so on. The important point was that the hub was acceptable to those who had not previously gone to church while the outposts and the outreach work meant that Christ was incarnated into the community, indeed, into some of the most deprived and most evil parts of London. No wonder Christ Church earned the title, the Nonconformist Cathedral.

Meyer Tries to Leave

Having already informed the church officers, Meyer wrote a letter to the Christ Church congregation, on 30 September 1901, of his intention to resign the pastorate in September 1902, by which time he would be fifty-five and would have completed ten years at the church and thirty-five in pastoral work.

The reason he gave was that 'Neither nervously nor physically can I bear the severe and constant strain which is involved in such a Pastorate, together with the outside work to which I feel I am specially called.' He added that it was better to give up 'while our congregations are larger than ever, and the whole organisation thoroughly healthy.'

Even more than in Leicester, Meyer was under 'severe and constant strain'. Consider a typical weekend. On Saturday afternoons it was his habit to give a talk to, and spend time with, young men at the YMCA in central London. At 7 p.m. he would conduct the workers' prayer meeting, that is for the many volunteers, before moving on to the Pleasant Saturday Evening, which drew young men and women, or the gathering for families. On Sundays he would usually preach at three services and, no doubt, would participate in one or more of the four or five meetings for children and young people. The church was open for tea for anyone from 4 p.m. and Meyer welcomed the opportunity of meeting members and newcomers in an informal way. No wonder Meyer lived at the church over the weekends.

During the week, Meyer was likely to lead the Women's at Home on Monday afternoons and the church prayer meeting in the evening. On Thursdays he conducted a lunch-time service and on Friday evenings there was a Bible reading (later taken on by the Revd A. Evans). If it is added that Meyer might well have had two engagements on Tuesdays and Wednesdays, he must have been giving at least nine sermons or talks per week.

There was more. He had the oversight of all the agencies based on and stemming out of Christ Church and he clearly kept in close touch with them. No doubt, he had regular meetings with the church elders. He founded the South London Missionary Institute and had to devote some time to its administration and teaching. He also lectured at the East London Missionary Institute. He gave time to the temperance and purity movements. Tuesdays and Wednesdays might well involve much travel – he sometimes left at 5 a.m. for places like Plymouth or Glasgow when he spoke at campaigns and conferences. He did have other times away which involved speaking at Keswick or abroad.

Somehow he found time to see individuals, to prepare his talks and to write books. He had twenty-five books published in the ten years between 1892 and 1902. No doubt the material for his talks went into his books but it was still an astonishing number. Not least, Meyer maintained his personal prayer time and Bible study, apparently by rising early in the morning.

In his mid-fifties, Meyer was feeling the pressure. Simultaneously, opportunities for what he called his 'wider ministry' continued to be placed before him and he was keen to travel at home and abroad 'to quicken and raise the standard of Christian living'. Indeed, despite the strain, he could not stop travelling. In early 1902, he and his wife went to Russia and he addressed twenty-four meetings plus a number of gatherings in people's homes.

Meyer would do nothing to damage the church. So he added a kind of 'let out' clause to his letter. He wrote that if Christ Church could not find a suitable successor 'I will gladly retain the <u>nominal</u> (Meyer's underlining) pastorate till the church is settled.'

In effect this is what happened. Efforts were made to make him reconsider his decision but he insisted. However, Christ Church could not find a man it deemed able to follow Meyer. Dr. A. Pierson, an American, well-known to Meyer through his friendship with Moody, acted as caretaker minister for two spells, in which his main duties were to preach while the Revd A. Evans oversaw the running of the church and its organisations. Interestingly, in a letter to Evans from Sweden in October 1902, Meyer said he was glad to hear that Dr. Pierson was moving to change the nature of the Sunday evening service. Evans moved to head up another church in 1903 and was succeeded by Mr. F. Iredell for a year and then by the Revd E. Reed.

During this period, Meyer was mainly occupied outside. He travelled widely and spoke in Scandinavia, Germany and Jamaica. He became involved with the Welsh Revival and, in his unpublished *Memories of a Long Life*, tells about his attendance at meetings which preceded it. At one, at Llandrindod in 1904, both he and Pierson gave stirring addresses (as did several others whom Meyer does not mention) which led to a midnight prayer meeting at which ministers 'consecrated themselves afresh to God and definitely asked that the Lord would raise up someone who would usher in and guide the Revival'. There followed the great revival of 1904 to 1905 led by Evan Roberts. Meyer rejoiced to hear of it and hastened to be present.

Meyer was still a part of Christ Church and, following Pierson, did at last introduce the non-liturgical evening service. He had his office at Christ Church and a salary. But his wider ministry had already started and his final letter of resignation came in 1907. On 18 April, he wrote to his friends that he was to 'step down from the pulpit of Christ Church'. He noted that, since he had been freed from his everyday duties at the church, it had been increasingly pressed upon him that he should become 'a sort of Bishop of the Free Churches throughout the country'. He said that he would be continuing as the landlord of the Nelson and that he would have a room at 80 Oakley Street where Sister Margaret continued with her work. Meyer called it his 'Passive Resistance house' and it appears his campaign against the Education Bill (which will be explained later) had its headquarters there. The cutting of the Christ Church tie meant he lost not just his office but also his salary.

The dates at the head of this chapter for Meyer's years at Christ Church are 1892 to 1907. Meyer did not officially leave the church until 1907 but his wider ministry really began in 1902. So the dates of the next chapter, in order to accommodate the overlap, are given as 1902 to 1909.

6

FREE CHURCHMAN AND BAPTIST
1902–1909

'The wider ministry'

Born and bred a Baptist, F. B. Meyer gradually found the confines of one denomination a limitation to his ministry. While at York, he met evangelist Dwight Moody who would preach almost anywhere to reach the lost. His growing interest in missionary work drew Meyer into contact with missionary societies, like the China Inland Mission, which recruited missionaries from any kind of evangelical background. Meyer began to associate with ministers from other Nonconformist denominations like Congregationalists, Presbyterians, and the various kinds of Methodists. His attachment to the Keswick convention under the banner 'All One in Christ Jesus' put him on the speakers' platform with Anglican ministers who had tended to dominate the convention. As he became known to other denominations, so Meyer received increasing numbers of invitations to speak all over Britain and abroad. From 1902 he was concentrating on this 'wider ministry' in which he was not limited to one church and one denomination.

Meyer and the Anglicans
Meyer's introduction to the Keswick Anglicans had started with some mutual suspicions. Like Meyer, the Keswick members of the Church of England were conservative evangelicals but they

had doubts about his 'social gospel'. On Meyer's part there was a doubt about the foundations on which their church was built.

In the 1890s, that is after he was an established Keswick speaker, Meyer wrote a series of articles, published as a twopenny booklet entitled *The Book of Common Prayer. The Ground for Religious Nonconformity*. In it, he acknowledged the debt to political Nonconformists who had struggled, even died, to win the civil rights which had been denied to those who did not conform to the established church. But he made it clear that he wrote as a religious Nonconformist. He did not object to the use of the liturgy, to the union with the state, with the maintenance of an episcopal method of church government. He respected many Anglican clergymen past and present. He was a Nonconformist because of his 'religious and conscientious objection to the Book of Common Prayer'.

Meyer explained that Church of England clergymen had to accept three main articles within the Book; the royal supremacy in spiritual as well as temporal things; that the Book of Common Prayer contained nothing contrary to the Word of God; and that the 39 Articles likewise were in agreement with the Bible. While agreeing that much of it was in accordance with Scripture, Meyer identified parts which were not, such as the assertion that infant baptism made a child 'an inheritor of the Kingdom of Heaven', that priests were superior to other Christians in being able to absolve sins and in officiating at the Lord's Table, and that those who did not hold the creed would perish everlastingly. In addition, he saw no grounds for accepting the spiritual supremacy of the monarchy – indeed he called some of the previous kings 'unmitigated scamps'.

Unlike some Nonconformists, Meyer did not want continual spiritual war with the Church of England. He had laid down the reasons why Nonconformists could not and should not seek organisational unity with it. He was prepared, however, to co-operate with individual Anglicans who loved and followed the Lord Jesus Christ. Indeed, Meyer insisted that a 'mystical union' existed between all true Christians. It was in one of his holiness books, *The Dedicated Life*, that he wrote that the reader might differ markedly from a friend, 'He is a Radical, and you Conservative; he is a Democrat, and you a Republican; he is an Episcopalian, and you a Methodist; he is inclined to Mysticism and you to Pragmatism. But there is this point of contact, that you are one in Christ, members of His body, of His Flesh and Bone.' This mystical unity between individuals did not mean agreement on all matters between the churches. Indeed, as will be shown, Meyer was to object strongly to attempts by the established church to take public funds for their schools. But Meyer still maintained personal love and respect towards its individuals.

Perhaps even more surprising was Meyer's attitude towards Roman Catholics in an age when differences between Protestants and Catholics were still major battlegrounds. Meyer certainly did occasionally preach against Roman Catholic doctrines, particularly the position it gave to Mary. Yet when, in 1893, a journalist asked him, 'Do Papists oppose you?' he replied, 'Not at all; and for myself I would not lift my finger to oppose them while there are so many people about here unsaved. First let us convert all the unsaved around here, and then I will see about fighting the Papists.' He expressed admiration for a Roman Catholic bishop whose devotional life served as a 'rebuke' to his own. While at Christ Church, he helped form a Public Morals Council which drew together a range of denominations including Roman Catholics and Jews. In short, Meyer preferred to spend his time on practical evangelism and social campaigning rather than on theological debates.

The Free Churchman

Meyer felt closest to evangelical churches in other Nonconformist denominations. He included under the Nonconformist or free church umbrella not only Baptists, Congregationalists, Presbyterians and Methodist, but also the Quakers. He had been influenced by grandmother, Ann Sturt, and he wrote an article about some of the seventeenth century Quakers or Friends. He referred to their 'deep spirituality – love, joy, peace, long-suffering, gentleness, goodness, faith, meekness, temperance'. Robert Wilson, one of the founders of Keswick, was a Quaker. Meyer did not push for amalgamating the Nonconformists into one denomination. Yet he wanted more than co-operation between individual churches and more than mystical unity between their individual Christians. He favoured a federation.

He played a part in strengthening the Evangelical Alliance, and spoke at its tenth international conference in London in 1896, but he put most energy in the 1890s to bringing the Nonconformist denominations into the Free Church Council, in order to promote joint evangelism, fellowship and common concerns. In 1897, its paper *The Free Churchman* was launched with Meyer as its co-editor. In an early issue he wrote that the mission of the Free Churches was 'to witness to the principles of self-sacrifice, righteousness, and brotherhood, in the hope of stirring the national conscience, and raising again a noble mission for great moral issues'. He continued that these issues included the excess of drinking, the growth of materialism, 'the shameful methods adopted in too many cases towards the native races of our great dependencies' and the increase in sacerdotalism. By the latter, the only item in his list aimed against other denominations, he meant the belief that ordained priests had powers and privileges which were considered superior to those of other Christians. Another issue he often mentioned was the condition of those women who endured 'weary days at labour utterly repulsive and nauseous to all refined instincts, where in some cases the work of two hours or more means a wage of twopence-halfpenny'.

As the number of local Free Church Councils multiplied so Meyer became president of the Metropolitan Free Church Council. By this time he was free for his wider ministry and was elected the national president for 1904–1905. Politically this suited Meyer for, historically, Nonconformists had tended to support the Liberal Party, with a special liking for William Gladstone. His presidential year also occurred while he was embroiled in public resistance to the Conservative government's education policy, as will be described below. Perhaps because of this, at his presidential address in Newcastle, he placed more emphasis on spiritual aspects, saying that the duties of the Free Churches were 'the training of the young, keeping the spiritual aspects of our work well to the front, securing a higher standard of Christian living, maintaining a closer fellowship with the Spirit of Jesus Christ and seeking a new endowment of power'. His vision was of a spiritually-alive church which also promoted national righteousness. Even when his presidency was completed, Meyer continued as a force with the Free Church Council and often spoke on their behalf in the following years.

During the first decade of the twentieth century, Meyer was at the heart of the Free Church Council. His talents for public speaking, writing and organising were used to the full as a national leader of the churches. He addressed hundreds of meetings where, as usual, he had a huge impact. He wrote numerous articles and was frequently interviewed by the press. He organised the Free Church Council, setting its strategy, making sure it was administered efficiently and raising money. He travelled all over the country, usually by train and often overnight. According to H. G. Saunders, who took over the editorship of *The Free Churchman* and often accompanied Meyer, the train became his office. He explained that once settled in a carriage, Meyer would 'open his dispatch case which was fitted up as a sort of stationery cabinet, and set to work in supreme contentment on some abstruse article quite oblivious of his surroundings'. He might then have a short sleep and be refreshed on arrival for the next meeting.

Meyer revelled in his Free Church role. It enabled him to popularise his views of the whole gospel. The Free Churches stood for evangelism, holiness and social action. In 1908 he proclaimed, 'Do not argue about the great principles of Christianity, but live them.' This meant applying them to individual life styles and collective action. Further, it gave him a platform to continue and extend two of his life-long concerns, temperance and social purity. Notably when a government Licensing Bill proposed to award compensation to brewers and publicans who lost their licences following official intervention, Meyer was quick to protest that public money should not be used 'to compensate those who had grown rich by the impoverishment of millions'.

Meyer now had growing confidence in himself as a political figure. This came because he had the backing of the Free Church Council, which was a body of national importance. As Randall puts it, he became 'the personification of the Nonconformist conscience'. Meyer was on the public stage.

The Public Figure
In 1902, Meyer became embroiled in a long-running national struggle which was both secular and religious. It stemmed from the Education Act of that year.

In 1870, legislation established School Boards in England and Wales to provide public funds for schools. It was understood that religious teaching would not be sectarian or denominational. Of course, numbers of voluntary schools run by the Church of England and, to a lesser extent, by the Roman Catholic Church continued. However, some Anglicans considered that the state religion should be taught at state schools and, in the 1890s, a number of candidates in the elections for places on the London School Board stood on these grounds. They were defeated but a writer, not Meyer, in *The Free Churchman* warned of battles ahead. He was right.

In 1902, the Conservative government passed its Education Act. The historian Sir Robert Ensor wrote that it 'ranks for England and Wales among the two or three greatest constructive measures of the twentieth century'. The reason was that it abolished the limited School Boards and shifted their responsibilities to county and county borough councils, that is put them fully under the local authorities, and set up some secondary schools. However, as well as the state schools, it also put voluntary schools run by the Church of England and the Roman Catholics into the scheme so that they too could be supported by local rates.

Nonconformists objected strongly, not to the Act as a whole but to contributing, via their rates, to schools run by other denominations. They were aggrieved that in rural areas, where the church school was sometimes the only school, Nonconformist children would have to attend it. Inside the Commons, the Liberal Party, particularly David Lloyd George, then a backbencher, objected. Outside, opposition was led by the Baptist, Dr. John Clifford.

Meyer was initially reluctant to enter the fray for fear of damaging his good relationships with individual Anglicans and not wanting a denominational battle. He had worked closely with the Bishop of Southwark on temperance and purity matters and he did not wish to harm that alliance. After all, he had endorsed the view that they were all one in Christ Jesus. He attempted to act as a mediator between Nonconformists and Anglicans, including his Keswick colleague Prebendary Webb-Peploe, a Conservative who supported the Act. Meyer failed and then swung strongly behind the opposition and denounced the Conservatives in no uncertain terms. He had long backed the teaching of the Bible in schools providing it was not used for denominational advantage. He now stated that it would be better to have no scriptural teaching than have it in the hands of Anglicans.

The Free Churches tried to develop strategies to stop the Act being implemented. On 23 May 1903, Meyer participated in a rally in Hyde Park with an estimated 140,000 protesters. The lead speakers included John Clifford and the Congregationalist, Sylvester Horne, but the loyal Fullerton observed how distinctly Meyer's speech could be heard in the great mass.

The rally did not alter the government's mind. The next ploy was passive resistance, in which protesters would withhold from their rates the amount they estimated went to church schools. Meyer had previously taught that Christians should uphold the law, pay their taxes and obey the authorities. He now altered his position and, in his later book, *The Dedicated Life*, he argued that disobedience is justified when the government's demands are clearly unchristian. He wrote, 'When Caesar ... demands things which are not his, but God's then another principle steps in, and we are bound to refuse to give to the earthly ruler that to which he has no right.' To Meyer, contributing to Anglican schools was such a demand.

Meyer had a rented house in Lambeth which he used as an office and sometimes for accommodation. He refused to pay the full rate and in September 1904 was summoned to the Lambeth Borough Court. His arrival at court was accompanied by enormous publicity, which was just what he wanted. In his papers there is a somewhat fuzzy photograph, cut from a newspaper, of Meyer in court. It is not known how it was taken for photography was forbidden at a trial. Meyer was soon on his feet and a religious journal reported that 'He spoke nobly and looked noble.' He may have looked noble but his speech was a kind of sermon about saving children from Anglicans and Roman Catholics. The magistrate cut him short and he was fined. The legislation was not changed but the protesters, of whom Meyer was a senior figure, had put the views of the Free Church on the public agenda.

With the 1906 general election approaching, Meyer turned his attention to party politics. He had previously written that ministers should encourage their followers to participate in politics but should not publicly advise them for which party to vote. Now he campaigned actively on behalf of the Liberals. His justification was that they were the party prepared to reverse the Education Act, but he was also enthusiastic about the Liberal-proposed programme of social reforms including old age pensions, school meals, compulsory insurance for certain categories of employees against illness and unemployment, and improved housing for working class people. Meyer, once again, called for improved work conditions and wages for women in unskilled and unpleasant jobs.

The Liberals, under Sir Henry Campbell-Bannerman, gained a landslide victory. The Conservatives lost half their seats while the fledgling Labour Party made its presence felt by winning twenty-nine seats. Meyer certainly rejoiced in the result (and with the fact that the number of Liberal MPs who were Baptists rose to eighteen) and declared that he was pleased 'that I had a hand in helping the government to office. ... I feel that the destinies of the country are in the hands of men in whom high moral works and brilliant statesmanship are blended to a quite surprising extent.'

The in-coming Liberal government did introduce a new Education Bill which dealt with some of the Nonconformist grievances. It was introduced by the President of the Board of Education, Augustine Birrell, who was the son of the Revd Charles Birrell and who had been a friend of Meyer's in his first pastorate in Liverpool. The bill fell to amendments, apparently influenced by the Church of England, in the House of Lords. The following year, Birrell was moved to be the Irish Secretary and, although two further attempts were made, the legislation was never passed.

Meyer turned his attack on the peers, whom he accused of putting class interests before the will of the people. Simultaneously, he was anxious not to overplay his political hand in case it gave the impression that these were the only cards played by the Free Church Council. In a number of speeches, he emphasised that evangelism and holiness were central to its purposes.

F. B. Meyer was not the only Baptist to be prominent in urging social reform. John Clifford of Westbourne Park Baptist Church was just as, if not more, well-known. Indeed, in the passive resistance campaign, Clifford (along with 190 others) was sentenced to prison for refusing to pay his fine for non-payment. Nor was Meyer the only evangelical to put pressure on political parties. Kathleen Heasman points out that a number lobbied Campbell-Bannerman and his cabinet to implement its promises concerning old age pensions. By 1909, payments of five shillings a week were being made to those of seventy and above whose income was below a certain level. Some Baptist ministers were more radical than Meyer. J. C. Carlisle identified closely with striking dockers in 1889. During the rail strike of 1911, Clifford proposed a legally-enforced minimum wage while Meyer called for prayer, arbitration and assistance for the strikers' dependents. However, part of Meyer's importance was that he also acted as a bridge with those evangelicals who were still suspicious of the social gospel. His reputation as an evangelist and his many books on holiness served to convince some that the gospel of social justice was a part of the same creed as that of ensuring that people were justified before God.

But he did not convince all evangelicals. Following his calls for passive resistance in 1903, there were rumours that the Keswick convention was dispensing with his services. Not so. On 20th July Meyer was in Leicester speaking about the education struggles and the next day was addressing 3,000 people at Keswick. Given that the leading and revered Keswickian, Prebendary Hanmer William Webb-Peploe, was supporting the Conservative Act, it was difficult to see how action could be taken against one and not the other. Some criticisms were also made of his campaigning for the Liberal cause in the 1906 election, in which he attacked Anglican supporters of the Education Act. At Keswick that year, Meyer apologised if he had unintentionally hurt any Anglican clergy. His apology appeared to be accepted by the convention but some individual Christians did show their disapproval. One former admirer sent Meyer a highly critical letter along with three of his books saying he did not want a Meyer book in his house. He was not alone and Meyer told a reporter, 'It is true that I have lost nearly one third of my former readers.'

The Baptist

Meyer's relationship with the Baptist denomination was complicated. But by the beginning of the twentieth century, certain strands can be identified.

He believed strongly in 'believer's baptism'. He disliked the term 'adult baptism' as he argued that young people and children could choose to be baptised. He contrasted it with infant baptism, which was conducted at the request of parents. In his booklet, *Seven Reasons for Believer's Baptism*, he argued that the act of baptism was in obedience to the example and command of Jesus Christ. He insisted that baptism did not make people Christians. Rather it followed conversion and was a public witness that the person had become a Christian.

He placed importance on baptism and practised it in Christ Church, which was an independent church. He even baptised some Anglican clergy there.

None the less, in his papers he kept an article by himself arguing that Christians could become a member of a Baptist Church without being baptised. My reckoning is that the article was published during his first ministry at Regent's Park Chapel.

He seemed to place more emphasis on members attending the Lord's Supper (or Communion). In an article in the *Christian Treasury*, a magazine which he edited for a while, he wrote a long piece on The Lord's Supper in which he urged Christians to partake on a weekly basis. He wrote, 'It occupies a very special and important place in the economy of the inner life. No amount of meditation or prayer can quite compensate for our neglect of this precious rite. ... It is a blessed and healthful means of grace, when taken not as a piece of dead formalism, but as a channel of communication between Christ and the soul.'

Meyer experienced some tensions about his position as a loyal Baptist and his wish to be an active Free Churchman. In 1905 he declared, 'I am a Baptist first ... there is no man who has been truer to our great principles than myself.' Yet writing in 1926 in the *Christ Church Jubilee Book* he stated, 'Let no voice, however persuasive, and no advantage, however alluring, induce the future leaders of Christ Church to ally themselves with any ecclesiastical denomination or movement.' Meyer was a Baptist *and* a Free Churchman, he was denominational *and* inter-denominational. He supported both strands. Moreover, he was often active for the Free Church Council and the Baptist Union in the same weeks or even the same days. This makes it impossible to separate out his Free Church and Baptist involvement in a neat chronological order.

President of the Baptist Union

The Baptist Union, formed in 1813, struggled for some years, then grew more steadily as Baptist churches settled some of the differences between themselves and saw the value of being linked in a union – as long it did not control them. Meyer's closer ties with the Baptist Union owed much to its secretary, John Howard Shakespeare. Born in 1857, his own father had been a Baptist minister. He spent some of his teenage years attending Belvoir Street Baptist Church in Leicester and sometimes went to hear Meyer. Shakespeare trained at Regent's Park College before taking his only pastorate in Norwich. In 1898, he was appointed secretary of the Baptist Union. He had a reputation as an autocrat who got things done. Despite periods of ill-health, he oversaw the money-raising project which led to Baptist Church House being established in Southampton Row, London as an impressive headquarters. He took over *The Freeman* and turned it into *The Baptist Times and Freeman* (usually known just as *The Baptist Times*) and was the moving spirit of the Baptist World Congress of 1905 which conceived the Baptist World Alliance. Clearly he wanted a more centralised, more effective and more public Baptist Union. He had observed Meyer's achievements at Christ Church and his leadership of the Free Church Council. The two men had much in common for both liked to keep a tight grip on their organisations. They formed what Fullerton called 'a very close friendship'. There were differences. Meyer favoured co-operation between denominations whereas – although he did not reveal it until later – Shakespeare favoured organisational unity even with the Church of England. Moreover, Shakespeare did not have a high opinion of the Free Church Council. These differences never stopped their friendship.

Shakespeare was so keen to have Meyer as president of the Baptist Union that its paper *The Baptist Times* campaigned on Meyer's behalf which, according to Ian Randall, broke its own rules about being neutral over nominations for offices. In May 1905 – when Meyer was not the minister of a Baptist church – he was elected vice-president and therefore president-elect to succeed Judge William Willis.

When the result was announced, Meyer joked on the platform that he was the prodigal coming home. In an immediate interview with the Christian press, he answered a question, about whether he wanted the end of denominationalism, by saying that he wanted the end of rivalries but not the elimination of denominations. He added, 'I think that various aspects of truth stand out ... when distinct bodies of Christians, without denying what is true in the case of others, affirm them.' This was a clever statement which would have calmed the fears of some ministers who already suspected the direction in which Shakespeare wanted to go.

Since 1900, the treasurer of the Baptist Union was Herbert Marnham (who continued in the post until 1935). A layman, Marnham was both a successful stockbroker and also the long-serving Sunday School superintendent at Heath Street Baptist Church in Hampstead. A liberal giver to good causes and a member of a number of public committees, he was a modest man who declined the honours usually bestowed on such figures. He was a capable treasurer and the combination of Meyer, Shakespeare and Marnham made a formidable trio at the top of the Baptist Union.

In the spring of 1906, Meyer delivered his presidential address at the City Temple in London. In a speech of over an hour, only the main points can be mentioned. He stressed that he wanted a renewal of the Holy Spirit throughout the Baptist denomination. He insisted that women must play a part in this and recorded his pleasure at the increase in the number of Baptist deaconesses. He was moving towards the radical position of women becoming Baptist ministers.

Turning from the spiritual to the social, Meyer declared, in a phrase he used more than once, 'that commercialism has had its day' and that society should be moving in the direction of co-operation rather than competition. Meyer was speaking still in the glow of the Liberal triumph in the general election. Once again, he spoke of the inadequacy of women's wages with working girls earning an average of ten shillings a week. He added that some Christians drew handsome dividends from the profits made by firms which treated their female staff badly.

He continued that it was all very well to promote missions for the fallen but it was better to deal with the conditions that made them fall. Putting it another way, he explained that as much sin stemmed from bad environments then the environments should be changed. He was now firmly of the opinion that help to individuals and welfare by the churches, although welcome, was insufficient and that Christians should be calling on government to introduce legislation to tackle poverty and injustice. This involvement of Christians in the world did not make them less spiritual and he summed up, 'We must specially discountenance any attempt to divorce spiritual religion and politics.'

Meyer concluded by specifying the duties of the churches, which were to teach the sacredness of all life, to uphold Christian standards in a Christian nation, and to press the ideals of the Sermon on the Mount upon all social classes.

When he sat down 'the reception accorded him was magnificent. Cheers echoed and re-echoed round the galleries as if they would never end.' These words were penned by a Meyer fan, Chester Mann. Nonetheless, the speech received enormous coverage in the religious press and made impact on the whole Noncomformist community.

In the company of Shakespeare, Meyer then undertook an extensive car tour of Baptist churches, especially in village areas. A report in the *Baptist Times* of 27 June 1906 gives a detailed account of one month in four counties in which they visited sixty different places and Meyer gave 120 addresses. Usually he started with an open air message before spending time with local Baptists.

Following the tour, Meyer made speeches in several cities. A constant theme was the poverty he had seen amongst Baptist ministers in villages. He complained that some were surviving on £60 to £70 a year for themselves and their families with numbers 'unable to afford more than a modicum of meat or coals, and are glad to pick up an extra-half crown'. Simultaneously, he played tribute to their work and witness.

In early October, Meyer attended the Autumn Assembly of the Baptist Union at Huddersfield attended by 1,400 delegates. He was in his element. At a reception, he responded with wit and warmth to a welcome from the mayor, Benjamin Broadbent, a strong Methodist, and then congratulated Huddersfield on the development of municipal socialism. Soon he was in the midst of a meeting protesting at atrocities by government troops in Belgian Congo upon native residents. Missionaries from there told of floggings and mass murder. Meyer seconded the resolution urging the British government to act independently if necessary to bring justice there. He also chaired business sessions and one report noted his good-humoured skill in enabling some speakers to keep their tempers under control.

In his address, Meyer stated his belief that the huge changes taking place in society were God-given and that Baptists had a responsibility to make sure the message of Jesus Christ and Him crucified was not left out. Nor should Baptists shun political involvement and he again attacked the House of Lords for undermining the government's educational proposals.

He continued that if Baptists were to play a full part in the new society then it needed not just a properly paid ministry but also a properly educated one. He wanted a Baptist university college. He poured scorn on those who sneered at colleges as 'just man-made institutions' and who looked upon culture and education as 'something inherently opposed to spirituality'. He reasoned that religion in the future could only be effectively taught as a part of universal life 'and for that teaching and far-reaching knowledge of life will be an indispensable requisite'. Meyer's comments about education did not come out of a vacuum. He was supporting Shakespeare, who was pushing for a better educated and qualified ministry.

A few days later, Meyer addressed the annual meeting of the Leicester churches at Melbourne Hall where he was delighted to learn that, under the leadership of Fullerton, the church was as strong, if not stronger, than in his time. But not all churches were like Melbourne Hall and he criticised respectable church people who welcomed working men at the door and then put them up in the gallery. He foresaw that working people would 'be the rulers of the state' so that it was essential that they were not estranged from the church.

Shakespeare was delighted with Meyer's year as president. He had attracted large audiences, drawn in more churches, and ensured a high profile for the Baptist Union in the Christian press and beyond. He was determined to maintain the close connections with him. On stepping down as president, Meyer continued to criss-cross the country to speak at meetings for the Baptist Union.

Meyer and Socialism

As noted, during these years Meyer made approving sounds about the values of socialism and the potential of the Labour Party to replace individualism by co-operation. The question arises, was Meyer a socialist? One paper sneeringly called him Comrade Meyer. It is useful to compare him with one of his contemporaries, George Lansbury, whose biography I have written.

Lansbury was born in 1859 and raised in London's East End. He emigrated to Australia to find work, returned disillusioned and campaigned to accuse emigration societies of publishing a false picture about prospects in Australia. His abilities aroused the interest of the Liberal Party which was seeking talented working class support. He became a successful Liberal election agent. Despite being promised a seat in the Commons, he left to be a socialist because of his conviction that only a working class movement would serve its interests. He went on to become an MP, cabinet minister and, in the 1930s, leader of the Labour Party. He never made a secret of his Christian beliefs and A. J. P. Taylor described him as 'the most lovable figure in modern politics'.

Lansbury and Meyer had much in common. They were both Christians and both supporters of temperance and purity organisations. Their political beliefs sprang from the Bible. Neither was unduly influenced by Karl Marx. More surprisingly, neither seemed to have absorbed Frederick Engels' classic *The Condition of the Working Class in England*. Their views on society owed little to economic analysis and much more to Christian values. Both wanted to build a more Christian society and considered that politics was one way of doing so. Both supported the

Christian Social Union which was founded in 1893 to consider how Christianity could be applied to social problems.

Both Lansbury and Meyer believed that poverty and want should not exist in a Christian society. They agreed that such evils could not be tackled just by individual charity and Christian agencies and that state provision was necessary.

There were, however, differences. Lansbury was an Anglican, Meyer a Nonconformist. Lansbury became a full-time politician intent on promoting a socialist society while still being involved in church life. Meyer was a full-time Christian minister whose social interests were just one part of his ministry.

Crucially, they differed over socialism itself. Lansbury regarded himself as a democratic socialist. He always said that his main task was to win people to socialism so that they elected a government which promoted equality through a radical redistribution of income, wealth and power. He did not want to abolish the free market but to have it under the control of the people. He did want the major industries – coal, steel, railways and the like – to be run by elected public boards. All of this had to be underpinned by fraternity, the living for the sake of, and in fellowship with, others. To Lansbury, socialism was the mechanism for promoting the Kingdom of God on earth, hence he was known as a Christian Socialist.

Meyer, in an interview in 1908, made his position clear. He specified parts of socialism with which he was in agreement, the most important being the following:

(1) that every life shall have a fair chance. (2) that the gifts of the Divine Father to His creatures shall be more equally distributed. (3) that voluntary co-operation is realised as a truer method of life than individualism, but it must be voluntary. Such a co-operation would leave ample scope for individual effort. (4) ... if a man is willing to work, work ought certainly to be found for him. (5) the community ought to benefit by the unearned increment.

Meyer then expressed his opposition to nationalisation, especially of capital. He wanted state bodies to abolish poverty, to provide work and decent housing. He seemed to have no objections to this being financed by taxation. Simultaneously, he was opposed to taking capital, the means of controlling industries, out of private hands. Given his commercial background, it is not surprising that Meyer valued private enterprise. Yet, interestingly, he did not believe that business people should 'make profit their main consideration'. A profit had to be made but the main objective 'is to do your best for your client', in short to serve him. Meyer was not a socialist but he was not the kind of capitalist who believed in the maximising of profits come what may. Again, he wanted a fairer distribution of money, but he stressed that this should be by voluntary action – which was much more likely to happen in a society which took the example and teachings of Jesus seriously. Unlike Lansbury, he did not want socialism if that meant wholesale public control and redistribution. He would certainly not have agreed with the Anglican, the Revd Conrad Noel, who flew the red flag over his church in Thaxted, Essex, and who, in his book, *Socialism in Church History*, attempted to show that God had created all resources to be held in common and advocated 'a commonwealth whose people should own the land and the industrial capital and administer them co-operatively for the good of all'.

For all his sympathies for Labour, particularly with its emphasis on co-operation, Meyer was never a member of the Labour Party. He was an advocate of and a practitioner of a social gospel which stemmed from his Christian beliefs. It led him to argue for some, but not overwhelming, state intervention. He saw that the free market resulted in poverty and severe inequality but he believed that humane legislation, Christian practices by owners of capitalism and provision by voluntary societies could address the problems. Even this made him a radical political figure in the eyes of some evangelical Christians. He remained a Liberal and his position was not that unusual. A number of Liberal MPs in agreement with some (but not all) Labour values and policies were known as Lib-Labs, whereas others were much more in favour of an unfettered free market. This split was later to cause serious difficulties for the party. But by that time, Meyer was in charge of a church again.

Trips Abroad

If Free Church, Baptist and public activities were not enough, Meyer was also making tours abroad in these years. As mentioned, in 1891, he made his first trip to the USA and was eventually to go there at least twenty times. Between 1891 and 1907, he also went to India, Burma, Aden, Somaliland, Syria, Russia and Italy and probably other places which I have not traced. Sometimes he was accompanied by his wife while at other times he would be away from her for months. More discussion of Meyer the traveller will be given in chapters seven and eight. Here it suffices to mention three of the pre-1907 trips followed by a longer account of his time in South Africa.

In 1898, Meyer crossed the Atlantic again. He went to Washington, opened the Senate with prayers and had a talk with President McKinley.

In 1898 to 1899, he undertook a strenuous lecture tour in India organised by the Students' Volunteer Movement. Within India, he travelled 20,000 miles, lectured in twenty large cities and, in all, made 120 addresses. He spoke mainly to Indian Christians through an interpreter but also to missionaries and to Indians of other faiths.

Interviewed on his return to Britain, Meyer identified three highlights. One was that in India, the Christians largely ignored denominational distinctions. Another was that, to his surprise, Indian women had strong social and religious influence. He attributed this partly to the development of Christian colleges to which high Indian officials sent their daughters. Meyer stated, 'In my opinion, it is this education and proselytization of the Indian women which, in the long run, will be the main factor in the conversion of the Indian peoples.' Lastly, he had talks with some Indians of other faiths and was impressed by their deep religiousness, charity, purity and self-denial.

In 1901, he was back in the USA and this time made his first visit to the southern states where he was appalled by the treatment of black people years after the American civil war.

South Africa (1908)

During his trip to South Africa from April to October 1908, Meyer sent regular reports and articles to the British Christian press. He used these as the basis of a book *A Winter in South Africa* which was published very quickly on his return.

South Africa was an important and rich part of the British empire. Between 1899 and 1902, the Boer War had been fought. The reasons were complex, involving commercial and political factors but, to simplify, differences between the Dutch Boers and British subjects who lived in South Africa resulted in what was essentially a war for independence. Britain itself was divided between a 'pro-Boer' element which wanted to avoid war – and, once hostilities started, to make peace – and the 'imperialists' backed by jingoistic public opinion. In the end, the Boers finally sued for peace. Both sides had lost thousands of combatants while the Dutch were left further embittered by the deaths, mainly through disease, of many civilians held in concentration camps.

Meyer, with his political interests, would have shared in the public interest in South Africa. In addition, British evangelicals had links with fellow Christians in South Africa. The purposes of the visit, which was at the request of the Free Church Council, were to encourage greater inter-denominational co-operation through South Africa's Church Councils and to encourage and strengthen Christians. In addition, Meyer had been appointed President of the World's Sunday School Association in the previous year and he was keen to observe the work of Sunday Schools in South Africa. By this time, Meyer had no pastoral commitments and said that his only regret at leaving Britain was that he could not give his support to a Licensing Bill, introduced by the Liberal government with the backing of Anglicans and Nonconformists, which was eventually defeated in the Lords.

Meyer and his wife travelled on the liner *Walmer Castle* from Southampton. Meyer loved sea travel, never suffered sea sickness and found time to read, prepare and rest. Once in South Africa, he went to at least eighteen cities and undertook his usual punishing round of several engagements every day despite being sixty years of age. He did succeed in promoting more co-operation between churches, including the Dutch Reformed Church, although he was critical of the Anglican clergy for standing aloof. He preached to large audiences about consecration and holiness and found opportunities for evangelism. He gave backing to his favourite temperance and purity movements and showed interest in YMCAs and Sunday Schools. He also touched upon a theme which has become popular in the present century, Christians and sport. Meyer met Paul Roos, the captain of the Springboks in their recent victorious tour of Britain. Meyer rejoiced that Roos and a number of his team went regularly to church and prayer meetings. However, Meyer would have regretted that white and black people rarely played together in South Africa. Of a previous visit to India he had written, 'When I was in India and saw the natives, Eurasians, and English joining together in lawn tennis and in cricket, I realised what a marvellous uniting force there was in these great public games, which break down differences of caste and blend men for the time at least into one.' This playing together may not have happened in all parts of India but it showed his desire to break down the barriers of race as well as class.

He had resolved not to take sides on political issues in the way he did in Britain. But his deep convictions and emotions meant he did not always succeed. He expressed some anti-war sentiments. Everywhere he saw memorials to the many who had died in the Boer War and heard horrific tales of torture and suffering. In his book, he urged readers to 'join with that ever-growing band of men and women who will never rest until war is no more and its apparatus shall be relegated to our museums with the specimens of a vanished geological age'. At one meeting, he criticised the practice of Sunday volunteering in which young men were pressurised to drill and learn about arms. Soon after, a leading South African, Lord Methuen, took issue with him and argued that it was necessary to be prepared, apparently in case of uprisings of native peoples. Meyer retorted that in any country where black people far outnumbered the whites it would be impossible to hold the country by force and that it was necessary to build a national morality which underpinned peace. As religion was the core of morality, it was regrettable that Sunday drilling drew men away from church.

In 1904, Meyer had criticised the British government for allowing South African mine owners to import Chinese people to work in conditions which he described as 'slave labour'. Now he saw racism at first hand. He was angered at the treatment by those of Dutch and British ancestry of what he called the coloured and native populations, the former being 'the mixture of the white and black races, while the latter denotes the pure blooded descendants of the original inhabitants of this land'.

Meyer made no secret of his disapproval of discrimination which meant that black people could not ride on the same trams as whites, could not walk in the parks or on the main pavements while few were allowed to participate in political life. He was 'indignant that any should speak of them as niggers, deserving only to be horsewhipped or killed'.

Not all white people shared these prejudices and some argued that black people should vote for their own assemblies, which should put forward proposals to the white legislatures. Meyer backed this view which might now be considered conservative but, as Randall points out, at the time it 'was very radical – too radical for conservative white opinion'. In fact, Meyer went further and, in his book, indicated that having their own assemblies was a stepping stone for 'only as they govern themselves can people become ripe for self-government'.

Meyer's positive attitude towards black people was reinforced by the deep spirituality and range of abilities he saw. In Natal, he attended a gathering of five hundred Christian Zulus where, at one session, representatives of their churches brought contributions to the mission which worked amongst them. He wrote, 'Out of their deep poverty, the abundance of their joy abounded unto the riches of their liberality.' He continued, 'I felt very much at home amongst these simple people. The same Divine Spirit which was in them was in me.'

At this time, the Natal government was proposing that native ministers should not be left in charge of churches or mission stations. Meyer criticised the proposals just as he took to task those who complained that educating black people – as many Christian missionary societies were doing – was a waste of money in that it just turned them into more efficient criminals. Meyer proceeded to list a number of studies which showed that education benefited the employment skills of black people and that very few of them committed crimes or went to prison.

Meyer's visit coincided with Mahatama Gandhi being in the news.

Gandhi had practised as a lawyer in South Africa for a number of years and was leading protests against a law to make Indians be thumb printed and to carry a certificate. In February 1908, he was attacked by a mob and rescued and nursed by a Baptist minister, Joseph Doke. Meyer knew Doke who introduced him to Gandhi and they had two meetings in Johannesburg. They discussed passive resistance, with Gandhi drawing upon Meyer's non-violent protests against the Education Act. They also discussed Hinduism and prayer. Meyer developed a respect for Gandhi and recorded, 'He has a great reverence for Jesus Christ, whose face arrests you on entering his office as it hangs over his desk'. Shortly afterwards, Gandhi was imprisoned, for the second time, for leading resistance to the law.

Meyer was so moved by Gandhi that almost immediately he wrote an article in the British press expressing his opposition to the requirements being placed on Indians which, he said, exposed them to 'needless humiliation and degradation'. He said that Gandhi was hoping to visit Britain and he would be glad to welcome him for 'I never met a man more sincere or so absolutely regardless of money.' He concluded, 'How strange it is that such men are regarded with such antipathy by many white people! Their souls are so pure and elevated that they are interesting and attractive in the extreme. Their minds also are so agile, their manners so essentially polite.'

From the letters he received and from coverage in the press, it is clear that Meyer was well received in South Africa, did strengthen many Christians and did lead others to put their trust in Jesus Christ. Yet he too was blessed and received what can be called his fourth turning point. One evening, he retired to his room with a deep sense of failure. As he searched for the cause, it was shown to him that 'it is impossible for the soul to have an experience of the Resurrection, Ascension or Pentecost unless it has first realised the subjective and inner meaning of the Cross.. ... It is not enough to say that Christ died for us; it is peremptory that each believer should take up his own cross; or rather, that each should see himself already, in the purpose of God, nailed to the cross of Christ. Thus a new element entered my preaching...'. Subsequent meetings were full of power and blessings. Meyer was delighted that on two successive Sunday afternoons, two thousand natives came to his open air addresses.

Meyer was never content to stagnate in his Christian life and was often examining the state of his own spirituality. This experience touched him deeply. Thereafter he identified with Christ's death in a deeper way than before and it became another central topic in his meditations, preaching and writings.

On arriving home, Meyer was interviewed in *The British Weekly* which had a wide circulation in South Africa as well as Britain. In it, he spoke of the welcome he had received from the Dutch who had said, 'You are the first Englishman we have welcomed to this church ... because you were our friend during the war.' This indicates that Meyer was in the pro-Boer, pro-peace minority at that time.

Further, he called a meeting with the Baptist South African Aid Society to explain that in South Africa a number of Baptist churches were crushed by debt. He proposed that British agencies should make loans to these churches at four percent interest as against the eight percent charged in South Africa and that a fund should be established for church extension work there. He promised to raise £1,000. Meyer had gone to South Africa under the auspices of the Free Church Council and spoken on its behalf but he had also pursued his Baptist interests. Meyer was nearly always simultaneously a Baptist and Free Churchman.

But he was about to become a Baptist minister again.

7

REGENT'S PARK AND CHRIST CHURCH REPEATED
1909–1920

'The pendulum swung again'

In 1909, Meyer accepted an invitation to return to Regent's Park Chapel as its minister. As Fullerton commented, 'The pendulum swung again.' It was an unexpected decision given that Meyer had left that church because he wanted to reach the masses and because he desired to be in a non-denominational church. The pendulum continued to swing for six years later he was back at Christ Church.

The Eastern Tour (March–September 1909)
The negotiations between Meyer and Regent's Park Chapel took place while he was abroad. After coming home from his strenuous time in South Africa in October 1908, it might have been thought that Meyer would have liked a prolonged stay in Britain. Far from it, within six months, he and his wife were off again by boat and train to take in Turkey, Bulgaria, Singapore, China and Japan. He went under the auspices of the Keswick Convention in order to spread its teaching on holiness. He was by no means the first speaker to represent Keswick abroad but it was a further indication that there was no deep split between Meyer and Keswick. He also went again in his role as President of the World's Sunday School Association.

Meyer sent copious reports to *The Christian* and *The British Weekly* and here only a few of his points can be mentioned.

In Turkey, he commented on the terrible cruelties and persecutions that had characterised that country and he expressed the hope that the promise of religious toleration would be observed, as stated in its new constitution which the Sultan had been forced to concede. He was encouraged by young Turkish Christians while, in Constantinople, he was thrilled to address three hundred Armenian women.

Bulgaria had recently gained independence from Turkey and was struggling to establish its economy. Meyer considered that the Greek Orthodox Church was dead. He was encouraged by fifteen Bulgarian pastors who travelled to see him. He held six private meetings with them 'explaining so far as I knew the deeper things of Christ'. They were so poor as not to be able to afford books and Meyer determined to start a book fund on his return to Britain.

On the Island of Penang, as in other places in the Far East, Meyer became aware of the sexual temptations to which European men were exposed. He wrote, 'I cannot say exactly what I mean, nor indicate the awful ravages wrought by sin. Rank after rank of young life is mown down by the pestilence that walketh in darkness.' He heard of the suicides of several young British men. In order to reach them, he held meetings in the Town Hall between 1.30 and 1.55 p.m., during what was called the tiffin break. Many came for his short, frank, direct talk and Meyer stated, 'These men's meetings would have made it worth while to take the journey.'

In Singapore, Meyer delighted in the large numbers who gathered for prayer at 6.30 a.m. In the afternoons – and to his pleasure under the banner 'All One In Christ' – he delivered eleven consecutive addresses on the teaching of Keswick. A committee was established with a view to inviting a Keswick deputation. In the evening, Meyer spoke in the theatre to large mixed audiences of all nationalities and religions.

Meyer was in various parts of China for three months. He predicted that it would be a world power. Overall, he met with 1,500 missionaries, many of whom had survived the Boxer revolution and atrocities. On observing how missionaries of all Protestant denominations, including the Church of England, co-operated for common work such as training and medical schools, Meyer declared, 'We have to go to China to learn the spirit of unity.'

The numbers and abilities of Chinese Christians made an impression on Meyer. He recorded that some missionaries were anticipating the day when they would be banished, leaving behind independent Chinese churches.

Meyer certainly drew in the crowds and his efforts were much appreciated. From Shanghai, the Revd Nelson Bitton wrote for *The Christian* about his meetings for men, saying, 'Mr. Meyer got home. His frankness, his straight-hitting, and, above all, his desire to awaken and enlarge the good that he believes may be found in all men, together with a winning sympathy, has made him in the last few days a most popular messenger of God to the men of Shanghai. ... It is difficult in the extreme to touch these men, and the ordinary methods of evangelism make more mockers than converts among them. Mr. Meyer has proved that he can reach where others have signally failed.'

Another missionary, the Revd W. Clayton, reported on a meeting for missionaries in Canton where 'All present gained a fresh vision of Christ and of our upward calling to be partakers with Him in His victory over the world in the fullness of the Spirit's power, and in His intercession for the world. We were led on to claim our inheritance, and possess the possessions.'

Once again Meyer had a tremendous work rate. Amongst his papers, he kept a printed programme of his five days in Smyrna. He had a timetable of eleven meetings, each of which was for a different kind of audience so that translations were made in Spanish, Turkish, Greek and Armenian. In between, he visited the theatre at Ephesus where, as told in Acts 19, the crowds shouted 'Great is Diana of the Ephesians.' In all, he covered over 10,000 miles and travelled back to Britain by Trans-Siberian Railway, which took fourteen days. Back in Britain in September, a notice in *The Christian* listed twenty-five towns in Britain where Meyer was due to speak in the coming weeks. It also contained a report that he would be occupying the pulpit at Regent's Park Chapel for three months. In fact, it was to be for much longer than that.

Intervention of J. H. Shakespeare

It appears that, in 1909, Christ Church put out feelers to see if Meyer was interested in returning as full-time pastor. John Howard Shakespeare of the Baptist Union saw his chance. If Meyer was to be a pastor again, he wanted him in a Baptist church. Regent's Park Chapel was in difficulties again, so why not a return there?

On May 17th, he cabled an emotional letter to Meyer on his Far East tour, urging him to take over at Regent's Park, which would identify him fully with the Baptist cause. He added that the Baptists were in a crisis of leadership because 'Maclaran has gone into retirement – Clifford will soon go. We have no other world name but yours.' Alexander Maclaren was considered the greatest Baptist preacher of his day and died soon after his retirement in 1910. John Clifford was an evangelical, who, like Meyer also proclaimed a social gospel – and continued to do so long after 1909.

Meyer also received a hand-written letter, dated May 24, from Sir Alfred Pearce Gould, an elder at Regent's Park, from which it is clear that his church had invited Meyer to their pastorate and that he had declined on the grounds that he did not want to make a decision while Christ Church was without a pastor. This may have meant either that Meyer was thinking of returning to Christ Church or that he wanted to help the church out during the vacancy. The main point of Gould's letter was to ask Meyer to fill their pulpit from October 1st to the time he was due to go on another visit to America.

Having received a letter from Meyer, Shakespeare wrote again on June 2nd and expressed concern that Meyer appeared to be wavering between Regent's Park or Christ Church. He wrote, 'My wife and I both feel that you are in real danger of playing with a great opportunity and that it is possible through a sentiment to avoid a duty.' He then listed a number of reasons why Meyer should go to Regent's Park. One was that the church was in difficulties. Another was that it could be a base for 'dealing with a class in professional London which no one else can touch'. Next Shakespeare reckoned that Meyer had ten years left to be the Baptist leader throughout the world. Then, and perhaps most powerfully, he stated that it was not possible 'to carry through our projects unless you are a minister of one of the great Baptist Churches and at the very centre of everything'. These projects referred partly to the next Baptist World Alliance but more to the proposed Sustentation Fund of £250,000 (an enormous amount) for augmenting the stipends of the worst-paid ministers. Lastly, Shakespeare argued that Meyer had rendered magnificent service to Christ Church and now he owed something to Regent's Park. He followed this with a hasty note dated June 4th, saying that he had heard that Meyer might be filling in at Christ Church for a month and this would 'make a most unfortunate impression on the elders at Regent's Park'.

The plea about the Sustentation Fund would have moved Meyer. After all, it was Meyer who, as president, had brought the plight of poor ministers to the denomination as a whole. If Shakespeare's remarks about world leadership were somewhat overblown, Meyer would have had to acknowledge that the Baptist Union did possess few leaders of his reputation. Not least, there were ties of affection between the two men. Shakespeare made use of them when he wrote, 'May I add that I need you. You do not know how much.' Fullerton, who knew them both, was of the opinion that it was Shakespeare who took Meyer to Regent's Park.

There were other factors. Meyer had no regular income, although he never put much store by money. As always, Meyer always relished a challenge and Regent's Park was certainly that. Just as important, he had missed being a pastor. In an interview soon after his tour, he said, 'Certainly my travels during the past few years have acted as a new incentive to service. One has felt in a sort of widowed condition. One has missed so much the consciousness that one belongs to a church and that a church belongs to oneself.'

In September, Regent's Park Chapel offered the pastorate to Meyer. In a handwritten reply dated 13 October 1909, he pointed out that, as President of the World's Sunday School Association, he had promised to tour the USA from the end of the month until February. He had also received invitations from China, Canada, Australia and Turkey. However, he had discussed these issues with the church officials and he concluded, 'I feel it is God's will for me to accept your invitation.'

Meyer's acceptance featured in the secular as well as the religious press. *The Manchester Guardian* (now *The Guardian*) in a long report commented, 'It is always a fine testimony to the abiding worth of a man's earlier ministry for the memory of it to elicit a repetition. ... He is the Archbishop of the Free Churches.' It added that, at Regent's Park, Meyer would be able to proclaim his distinctive message which was, 'Society is in a shocking state. ... A reformed society is to be realised by the agency of an inspired and quickened church.'

Regent's Park Chapel (1909–1915)
The challenge was real. Before he arrived, the church's handbook had acknowledged that 'the prospects for our church did not appear bright'. In the previous years, membership had been falling and the church appeared to lack leadership and purpose.

Once again, the sources contain little information about Meyer's time at Regent's Park. Mann passes over it in two lines while even Meyer in his voluminous writings has not much to say. After his return from the USA in 1910, he wanted to put the emphasis on evangelising in the neighbourhood. Meyer was in his sixties and could not have had the same energy as when in his forties, but he was strengthened by the appointment of an assistant pastor and the election of five additional elders. Of course, Regent's Park was not the same kind of neighbourhood as Christ Church and its middle class doors were more likely to be opened by maids than owners. There would not have been the same buzz on the streets which he had enjoyed. Meyer must have missed the masses and, at Christ Church, it was often those recruited from the masses into the Brotherhood who were best at street evangelism.

Randall concludes 'that during this period Meyer does not seem to have been able to mobilise the church for mission to the same degree as he had done in his previous pastorates'. True, but he did attract larger congregations and the membership increased. In 1913, seventy-five people joined the church, of whom forty-eight came by transfer from other churches and twenty-seven by profession of faith. Not bad for a man of his age. Many ministers would have rejoiced in that number of conversions, although Meyer was probably not satisfied.

Outside of Regent's Park

Meyer's achievements at Regent's Park may have been more limited than in previous pastorates but they were made while he was also doing extensive work away from the church. Shakespeare soon had his friend involved in Baptist Union matters. Almost immediately he was drawn into raising money for a Baptist seminary in Russia. He started the appeal at the autumn assembly in Glasgow in 1910 and the following year, at the Baptist World Alliance Congress in Philadelphia, he told delegates, with his not uncommon exaggeration, that it was the greatest thing Baptists had done for centuries. He seemed keen to visit Russia but the outbreak of hostilities stopped him.

By 1912 Meyer was leading the drive for the Ministerial Sustentation Fund. For a period, Shakespeare was ill but Baptist lay people lent their support, while Regent's Park contributed over £5000. The Baptist Women's League, which Shakespeare had helped to initiate in 1908, played a crucial role. Its energetic president, Mrs Russell James, galvanised it into action. David Lloyd George MP, a Baptist, now Chancellor of the Exchequer, gave his backing. Meyer travelled all over the country banging the Sustentation drum and sending regular reports to *The Baptist Times.*

Fullerton includes a description of Meyer at work at a gathering in Glasgow. After a short talk about the value and the needs of poorly paid Baptist ministers, he had the audience eating out of his hand. Promise forms were distributed and Fullerton records that, after Meyer read that the first form handed to him was for £1,000, 'There was a moment of surprised stillness and then a storm of applause. After that the atmosphere was electric.' Meyer commented on the small as well as the large amounts and when, at the end, the total reached £13,350, the audience broke into 'Praise God From Whom All Blessings Flow.'

The target of £250,000 was reached in 1914 and Meyer retained in his papers the programme of the Thanksgiving Meeting on 27 April, at the Royal Albert Hall. The chairman was another Liberal MP, the chief whip, Percy Illingworth. The main speakers were the Revd Campbell Morgan and Mrs Ethel Snowden, a campaigner for Votes for Women and the wife of the Methodist Labour MP, Philip Snowden. The combination of a prominent Liberal MP, venerable Congregational minister and a radical Christian woman, reflected different parts of Meyer's appeal.

The fund did lead to a minimum stipend for ministers and so abolished their penury. But Shakespeare insisted that only ministers recognised by the Baptist Union could benefit from the fund. In turn this led to lists of accredited ministers in districts under General Superintendents. Shakespeare had succeeded in establishing the Baptists as a nationally known and efficiently run organisation. But critics of his centralising tendencies could point out that in 1907, for the first time in living memory, the membership of Baptist churches in England and Wales actually fell. The implication was that concentration on the centre took attention away from local evangelism. By this time Meyer was too exhausted to join in any conflict.

All the time, Meyer was also engaged in Free Church activities. The secretary of the Free Church Council had been the Revd Thomas Law. His body was washed up from the sea and it was believed that he had committed suicide. He had been a friend of Meyer and had travelled to Southampton to see him off when he sailed to South Africa. In October 1910 Meyer, with what Fullerton called 'his usual knight-errantry', took over as honorary secretary until other arrangements could be made. Other arrangements took a long time and he continued in the post for ten years.

Meyer undertook a considerable amount of administrative duties for the Free Church Council. He also led public activities. He mobilised support for purity campaigns. In 1901, he had published *A Holy Temple*, a sexually-frank book for a Victorian clergyman. He warned men against the sin of masturbation and implied that sexual continence led to muscular Christianity. As mentioned, Meyer made much of the need for male purity in his tour of the Far East. On behalf of the Free Church Council, he campaigned successfully in 1911 to force a suggestive dance about Adam and Eve off the stage at the Palladium. The following year, he – and other religious leaders – supported MPs who were raising concerns that Britain was a centre for the white slave trade.

The public attention gained for purity matters was as nothing compared with the furore he provoked over a boxing match. In October 1911 the black American champion, Jack Johnson, was booked to fight Britain's Bombardier Wells at Earl's Court before a crowd of 10,000. Meyer, on behalf of the free churches, protested that it would aggravate racial tensions as it was being spoken of as a fight for white or black supremacy. When Johnson had fought a white opponent in the USA the previous July, it had provoked the threat of violence in the city where it was to be staged, to the extent that police had to confiscate firearms and hold likely troublemakers in custody. It was reported that, in other cities, black people had been attacked and even killed for shouting for Johnson.

Meyer also opposed the contest on the grounds of brutality. He declared that he had no opposition to boxing as a recreation – a declaration which prompted some Christians to criticise him on the grounds of compromise – but he argued that heavy-weight fights, which often led to knock-outs, were dangerous.

He produced evidence that, in one fight, Johnson had battered an opponent's face beyond recognition.

The huge publicity in the press drew out much opposition to Meyer as a puritanical spoilsport. One paper called him 'Meddling, Maudlin Meyer'. A rowdy crowd besieged Regent's Park Chapel. He was not one to back down and he was encouraged by numerous supporters, including the Archbishop of Canterbury, Randall Davidson, and the Labour leader, Ramsay MacDonald. Meyer lobbied the chairman of the London County Council which had granted the licence for the fight and sent a petition to the Home Secretary, Winston Churchill, who agreed that the fight should not take place. Even so, it still required a court ruling to place an injunction on the promoters and boxers to ensure that it did not do so. The disappointed ticket holders included thirty-eight clergymen!

Fullerton wrote, 'At a bound, Dr. Meyer became world famous.' Much of the press saw his victory as a blow for decency while a Scottish paper published a cartoon of Meyer knocking-out both fighters under which was the text, 'And I brake the jaws of the wicked, and plucked the spoil out of his teeth' (Job 29:17, KJV). After Johnson protested in one paper that Bishop Meyer had cost him thousands of pounds, the strongly Nonconformist Meyer wrote a witty reply which ended, 'Had you called me by even the choicest terms in the boxing ring I should have forgiven you, but a bishop!'

With elections expected – in fact two took place in 1910 – Meyer continued his political involvement. He no longer campaigned openly for the Liberals and said that the Free Church Council would back any party, including Labour, whose programmes were in line with its objectives. The December election left Liberals and the Unionists (Conservatives) with the same number of seats, Irish MPs numbered eighty-four and Labour forty-two. Incidentally, George Lansbury won a seat for the first time at this election. Meyer must have felt some satisfaction when the Parliament Act undermined the powers of the Lords to veto bills. He continued to call for decent wages for men and women and made forays into the sphere of education. Britain experienced a series of strikes between 1910 and 1912 in which Meyer was always on the side of conciliation. One of the most serious was the miners' strike of 1912 in which at least 850,000 men came out. Meyer urged relief for the miners. In the end, they won a minimum wage agreement. Simultaneously, Meyer gave the Free Church Council's backing to temperance campaigns, to evangelism and to the preaching of holiness. As always, his social and political activities went hand in hand with his more spiritual ones. They also meant that he had an enormous work load.

Christ Church (1915–1920)

In addition, Meyer was still travelling. He had sailed to the USA in 1910 and 1911 and the sinking of *The Titanic* in 1912 did not deter him from going again. At the end of 1913, the sixty-six year old Meyer collapsed in the pulpit. He rested for a while at the home of his sisters in Pembury and then proceeded to ignore medical advice to slow down and reduce travelling.

Following Meyer's illness, Regent's Park Chapel in April 1914 appointed Frederic C. Spurr as co-pastor, an appointment of which Meyer would have approved, for he knew and respected Spurr. The intent of the church appears to have been to ease the pressures on Meyer so that he could continue as its pastor. It was thus a surprise – and almost a replay of his previous departure – when Meyer suddenly accepted an invitation to go back to Christ Church. Sir Alfred Pearce Gould, the senior elder at Regent's Park, was an eminent surgeon and vice-chancellor of the University of London. He was not a man to be trifled with yet Meyer did not appear to have kept him well-informed.

Why Christ Church again? It did have an enormous place in Meyer's affections as the place where he had reached the masses and integrated working class people into the church. In addition, the church needed him. The minister at Christ Church from 1912 to 1915 had been the Revd Len Broughton from Atlanta, USA who had put the church into debts of over £8,000 with building alterations. Moreover, numbers attending had declined. Meyer could not resist.

So Meyer, who had gone to Regent's Park following the plea of John Howard Shakespeare that he needed a Baptist base, chose to spend his last pastorate in a non-Baptist church. It did not end his involvement with the Baptist denomination and he always claimed to be a loyal Baptist. He would have been pleased when his friend (and eventual biographer) Fullerton was elected president of the Baptist Union for 1917 to 1918. Similarly, he would have welcomed the Baptist Unions's intentions in 1919 to draw up plans to develop the deaconesses into a Baptist Sisterhood for, as the Baptist Union historian, Ernest Payne pointed out, the organisation 'had been started twenty years earlier by F. B. Meyer'. However, Meyer did not appear to participate in the major Baptist controversy in the nineteen-twenties when Shakespeare wanted re-union with the Anglican Church. Shakespeare, after further periods of ill health, including depression, resigned in 1925, and Meyer no longer had the same official and personal links with the denomination.

Mann and Fullerton give much less attention to Meyer's second period at Christ Church. The biography by Jennie Street does not go beyond 1902. Fortunately, Ian Randall provides some information.

Meyer's second ministry at Christ Church could not be the same as his first, not just because he was much older but also because much of it occurred during the First World War. None the less, he increased attendances and within three years he had halved the debt and cleared it completely by 1918. He focused on work with the young. The Sunday Schools attached to the Southwark Sunday School Society had broken ties with Christ Church after a rift with Broughton. Meyer, ever the reconciler, soon brought them back into the fold.

The First World War (1914–18)

The start of the war on 4th August 1914 was greeted with enormous enthusiasm – constant waving of Union Jacks and men flocking to join the forces. Meyer had been part of the anti-Boer War faction and, while in South Africa, he expressed horror at the needless suffering caused by war. In the years preceding 1914, he often spoke on behalf of the Free Church Council in favour of government peace initiatives.

But Meyer had never claimed to be a pacifist. In 1898, he had written that the nation should always seek peace but 'We do not seek peace at any price. The loss of national honour is a greater evil than war.' A year before the outbreak of the First World War, he wrote glowingly about patriotism stating, 'Patriotism is the legitimate child of Religion. Was there ever a keener patriot than Isaiah or Jeremiah?' He continued, 'On the whole, then, we are bound by the decisions of the Government under which we elect to live, subjecting our personal preferences and tastes to the general conclusion to which our Nation may be led.'

These words of Meyer seem to be preparing the way for his support for war. When it came, despite his previous pleas for peace, despite his belief that all Christians, including those of other nations, were all one in Christ, despite his own German ancestry, he backed the decision to wage war against Germany with some enthusiasm. Indeed, he claimed that it was a Christian war with God on the side of the allies. So did the Baptist Union, which declared that Britain was struggling 'to shatter a great anti-Christian attempt to destroy the fabric of Christian civilisation'. Later, Meyer rejoiced when the USA entered the war, calling it 'a glorious day when ... the United States of America and Britain entered into a holy compact in the presence of God.' He added that it would bring a speedier end to the war and advance its three objectives: the right of self-government to all states, a new emphasis on international relationships, and the creation of a League of Nations to make war almost impossible.

War or no war, Meyer was still the minister of Christ Church and had to keep its services going. The main drawback was that thousands of local men were in the armed forces. One figure puts 760 members of Christ Church as having enlisted, an enormous slice of the church's male members and supporters. It meant a shortage of volunteers in the clubs and societies. None the less, Meyer succeeded in keeping the church active and even making some growth. A programme for 1918 shows that, as well as Sunday worship and prayer meetings, the main emphasis was on the Young People's Institute and the Young Worshippers' League. In addition, the Brotherhood and women's meetings survived.

The war may have closed some of Meyer's doors but it opened others. He was in the heart of London where thousands of members of the armed forces were stationed, often while waiting for embarkation to the trenches. He soon perceived that lonely soldiers were often vulnerable to heavy drinking and seeking sex with prostitutes. He protested that the civilian and military police were taking insufficient action against these evils.

In conjunction with the YMCA, he obtained the use of its hostel in Waterloo Road as accommodation for servicemen and raised much of the money for it himself. Next he produced a paper, *The Service Messenger*, which contained small news items and the Christian message in a lively form. It was akin to the Salvation Army's present *War Cry*.

The departure and sometimes death of so many men often left financial problems for their wives and families. The government decreed that all would receive allowances but initially had no administrative machinery to deliver them and so they often arrived late. Moreover the allowances were small. Consequently, Meyer and his colleagues often dealt with cases of poverty. Further, Meyer was available to comfort those whose husbands and sons were killed in the fighting. He knew something of their grief as his only grandson, Leslie, was one of them.

People like myself, who experienced the London blitz between 1940 and 1941, may have thought this was the first time Britain was bombed. In fact, from May 1917, the German Gotha bombers caused considerable damage. London suffered most, with a school in Poplar being destroyed and eighteen children killed. Waterloo Station was hit, with considerable loss of life. No air raid shelters existed so Meyer flung open the doors of Christ Church. On October 11th, he distributed a letter to the neighbourhood inviting all those who had taken shelter to a series of short services at the church. By the time the last raid finished in May 1918, 1,414 civilians had been killed and 3,416 wounded.

Many servicemen came to worship at Christ Church and to Hawkstone Hall for rest, comfort and food, where 20,000 free teas were served and this at a time of food shortages. Some of the men joined the Brotherhood as associate members. When the war finished, Meyer wrote to them, as they left London, urging them to join local Brotherhoods.

Perhaps the most remarkable of Meyer's wartime activities – given his encouragement to men to fight – was his services to conscientious objectors. Probably his own experiences of passive resistance to the Education Act made him sympathetic. In addition, many of the objectors did so on religious grounds, including many Quakers for whom Meyer always had respect. But the opposition to Meyer's passive resistance was as nothing to the sufferings of those who refused to fight when male conscription into the forces became law. They were condemned and vilified by the population at large, subjected to imprisonment and cruel treatment. A good example of what one man went through is given in Arthur Marwick's biography of Clifford Allen, a member of the No Conscription Fellowship. Before a tribunal in 1916, he argued that as a socialist he believed in the brotherhood of all men and so would not participate directly or indirectly in the war. Once his appeal was rejected, he was taken forcibly to an army barracks where his refusal to obey orders led to a court martial and sentence of one year's hard labour. Once this was completed, the process was repeated with a further sentence. He was harshly treated, fed on bread and water and made to labour. His health broke down and a prison doctor diagnosed tuberculosis of the spine, partially brought on by having no seat but a small stool. Numbers of men died, some went insane. Later Allen was released in broken health, which prevented his taking up his intended career in politics and contributed to his early death.

Meyer, with other church leaders, urged the government to treat conscientious objectors more humanely. He became one of the very few outsiders invited to address the Meeting for Sufferers of the Society of Friends. He spoke with Herbert Asquith and with Lord Kitchener, the Secretary of War. His influence was recognised by the No Conscription Fellowship and, despite his age, he travelled to France where numbers of prisoners had been taken, apparently to be executed. He saw thirty-four men in the Military Barracks at Boulogne. The *Manchester Guardian* later stated that he played a crucial part in having their sentences commuted to ten years penal servitude.

In 1917, Meyer wrote a booklet, *The Majesty of Conscience*, published by the National Labour Press. It contained case examples supplied by Bertrand Russell, one of the leaders of the No Conscription Fellowship as well as Meyer's own Christian arguments about the rights of conscience. People like Russell had reservations about Meyer because of his staunch Christianity but they recognised that a booklet by him would reach a much larger readership.

Interestingly, after the war, Meyer addressed a meeting of the No Conscription Fellowship and urged those who had been in prison to propose changes to the whole penal system in order to make it less punitive and more rehabilitative.

Given Meyer's respect for conscientious objectors, it is surprising that he declined to speak alongside his fellow Christian, George Lansbury. In 1928, in his biography, Lansbury recalled that during the war he was asked to appear with Meyer and added, 'The Revd. F. B. Meyer refused to go on the platform with me; he objected to my pacifism and to my attitude towards the war.' The reason was probably not his pacifism but more likely his vigorous attacks on those running the war, which Meyer may have regarded as an attack on British soldiers. Perhaps Meyer did not know that in the East End of London, Lansbury too was active in helping the relatives of servicemen and that he participated in a successful campaign to raise allowances for wives and widows.

Last Years at Christ Church
In April 1917, Meyer's seventieth birthday fell upon a Sunday and he spoke to the Brotherhood on 'How to be Young Though 70'. At the evening service, his theme was 'Death Abolished'. He finished with these words, 'I trusted Him because of the testimony of

my parents and of my minister. Since then I have wintered and summered with Him ... and on this seventieth birthday this is my assurance – that He is able to keep that which I have committed to Him. We cannot wear Him out or tire Him, and our sin is no barrier against His love.'

His preaching remained powerful and in 1918 an article appeared in *The Onslow Herald*. Its reporter had heard Meyer years before and now returned. He noticed that, although it was the holiday month of August, the congregation was large. Meyer was now an old man with white, thin hair but 'his vigour and animation in the pulpit is remarkable', complete with his usual grace, humour and practical usefulness. Meyer must have been pleased for he cut out and kept the article.

In December 1918 Meyer wrote to all members giving thanks that the war was over. He urged them to witness to and serve the needy around them. He invited them to the New Year's Social Gathering and, given the continuing shortage of some foods, 'to bring sugar in your pocket and a lump or two in your heart'. Within a year, Meyer looked for his replacement. He heard Dr. William C. Poole speaking at Spurgeon's Tabernacle and immediately asked him to preach at Christ Church the following Sunday. Soon after, Meyer informed him, 'A voice has told me that I have met the man who is to be my successor.' And so it happened.

In June 1920, the church celebrated Meyer's ministerial jubilee, fifty years as a minister. It included a strawberry tea in Hawkstone Hall where he had initiated numerous projects. It must have given him particular pleasure to see so many former servicemen who had not only come back to the area but also to the church organisations, which were steadily reviving.

With Meyer's retirement announced, the church made him minister emeritus and put aside a vestry for his use. His last ministerial letter to members was handwritten by him (and copied) in December 1920. He said little about himself but was happy that 'our congregations and agencies are in first rate order'. He reminded them 'that all outward life and work must emanate from real and close friendship with our Saviour'. Then followed a typical Meyer PS, 'Don't forget the Church Social on January 2nd @ 6.30'.

By retirement, Meyer did not mean cessation of activity. Already, in 1920, he had been elected for a second time as the president of the Free Church Council. Nor was he to stop travelling.

8

THE LAST YEARS
1920–1929

'The evangelical comet of the age'

Ever since 1891, Meyer had spoken in numerous countries. Overall, his destinations included the following: Aden, Australia, Bulgaria, Burma, Canada, China, Denmark, Egypt, Finland, Germany, Greece, India, Italy, Jamaica, Japan, Korea, Malaya, Norway, Somaliland, South Africa, Syria, Sweden, Russia, Turkey and the USA. Some he visited more than once. In old age in Australia, a friend commented how tired he must get. He replied, 'My dear fellow, I love it, I love it.' No wonder *The British Weekly* described him as 'The evangelical comet of our age.'

Freed from church responsibilities, Meyer did not let up. Despite the advancing years, he continued to be active at home as well as away. This chapter falls into seven sections: Keswick abroad; Keswick at home; his increased support of missionaries; his last cause, Adventism; the question of his pessimism; his children's home; and the final days.

Taking Keswick to the World
From the time of their first meeting, Meyer and Moody became friends. Meyer became a frequent speaker at the Northfield Conventions organised by Moody. He was alongside the grieving Moody when his granddaughter died in 1899. Within a few months, Moody was also dead.

Moody did not invite Meyer to Northfield just for friendship's sake. He believed that America was strong on evangelism but weak on Christian spirituality. He wanted Meyer to bring the Keswick message of holiness. This was in 1891 when Meyer's books had already made him well-known in the USA. Meyer later claimed that 'It fell to my happy lot to be the first of the Keswick platform to present the subjective side of Christian experience' in the Americas. At that Northfield Convention, he spoke twice daily for two weeks and he did not disappoint. Chester Mann, who was at Northfield, recalled, 'His addresses left hundreds spellbound.'

Thereafter, Meyer not only returned to Northfield time after time but also toured much of the USA and Canada with the Keswick message. He picks out three places in particular. The Carnegie Rooms in New York, holding three thousand, where, he said, 'There was deep attention and power. Chicago, at a 'never-to-be-forgotten' meeting with a thousand ministers and students. Richmond, in the south where crowds waited behind 'to seek from God a fresh anointing of the Holy Spirit'.

What was meant by the Keswick Message? Some disliked the term but Meyer used it. In an earlier chapter, Meyer's own experience of receiving the Holy Spirit at Keswick was described. That continued as his – and many others' – message of how to be filled with the Spirit. In 1892, Meyer preached a sermon called 'The Pentecostal Gifts' which was reprinted in a Christian paper. He concluded by saying,

> When you first were converted ... you looked up into the face of Jesus, and you took by naked faith the gift of eternal life. So – listen, for this is the deepest thing I know, it is the deepest thing I could tell you – open your heart to God and believe that directly you are willing to receive, that moment God does fill your waiting and receptive nature with the Holy Ghost.

In short, receiving the Holy Spirit depended on faith in God and asking for the gift.

This did not mean that Meyer denied that the Holy Spirit was not at work in people's conversions. He never taught that, once filled, they would never sin again or that they would not need further experiences with the Spirit. Rather Christians had to repeatedly draw upon the Holy Spirit to make them more and more like their Lord. As Moody wrote of Meyer, 'There was no advocacy of sinless perfection, but a clear presentation of a life truly yielded to God and the privilege it afforded of living free from the bondage of sin.'

Meyer taught the Keswick experience in season and out of season. But there was more to its message. He, and other Keswick teachers, stressed the importance of the Christian's spirituality or inner life or personal relationship with God. In order to be close to God, in order to obey Him, in order to benefit from worship, in order to witness for Him in the world, they had to be strong in individual prayer, Bible study and meditation. Meyer sometimes called this walking with God. One of his most popular publications was entitled *Our Daily Walk* which was still in print in 1995. It consisted of short daily readings and covered themes like faith, fellowship, love, service, sincerity, and wakefulness.

Meyer usually preached from a text or Bible passage. Another favoured approach was to examine in detail the lives of Biblical characters. He did this in 1921 in Grove City, Pennsylvania. A minister who heard him said, 'He did not spend his time trying to prove that Joseph or Abraham were mere ideas, but rather in letting us see in them, and through them, the foregleams of Christ.'

These talks were often based on or led to his popular books about Biblical characters. For instance, in *Peter, Fisherman, Disciple, Apostle*, published in 1919, he argues that Peter, who had denied Christ, received the Holy Spirit after the resurrection in the company of the other disciples and thereafter was empowered to be the great apostle. He adds that this infilling came to Peter at least twice afterwards. Meyer then asks his readers – and his audience when he preached – 'Why not acknowledge that there is a blessing here which is yours by right?' He urges them to confess their sins and open their hearts to the Holy Spirit. But there is more. He identified Peter's subsequent leadership qualities as 'Passionate devotion to Christ, unfeigned humility and indomitable courage'. He encourages Christians to develop qualities which make them leaders whatever their spheres of living. The Keswick style was not to question the historical accuracy of Biblical people but rather to draw lessons from them in order to encourage Christians in their daily round.

In the USA, Meyer spoke to individuals as well as crowds. Three examples must suffice. In his unpublished *Memories of a Long Life*, he writes at some length about a well-known American minister, Dr. Wilbur Chapman. He was so depressed with his efforts that he wrote a letter of resignation to his church. While the ink was still wet, he read a newspaper report of one of Meyer's talks at Northfield containing his words, 'It is not what a man does for God that really counts, but what God does by and through him.' He tore up the letter and henceforth allowed God to be a channel of power through him.

They met and Meyer told him you can't breathe out unless you breathe in. At first, Chapman thought he was giving him hints on public speaking until he realised that he could not continue to give out in preaching 'unless there are times for the in-take of fresh love and power through fellowship with the Divine Spirit'. Some time later they spoke together at a gathering for a hundred and fifty ministers at an open air meeting in a forest. All sought the re-anointing of the Holy Spirit. Meyer claims that 'the result was that revivals broke out in many cities and towns'.

As a member of the council of Dr. Barnardo's Homes, Meyer was always pleased to meet those who had been brought up there. In the USA, he met the Revd Havergal Sheppard and they spent a day together where, Sheppard recorded, 'He revealed to me the charm and challenge of the risen life.' Later both attended the Baptist World Alliance in London in 1905. Sheppard tells that he spent a happy day with Meyer and his wife and then accompanied Meyer to Founder's day at Barnardo's Village Homes in Barkingside, where Meyer was one of the speakers. He presented Sheppard with a set of his Bible character books.

Frank Buchman was a student when he first attended the Northfield Conventions and heard Meyer speak. Buchman subsequently ran a home for underprivileged boys but resigned when the directors cut back on the money for food. His biographer Mark Guldseth commented that 'his health and spirit [were] broken by overwork and bitterness'. He went to Britain to seek Meyer at Keswick. He was not there but Buchman was blessed at a small gathering led by Mrs Jessie Penn-Lewis, who was to play a part in the Welsh Revival. He heard Meyer in London and asked him the secret of effective preaching. Meyer replied, 'Tell your people on Sunday the things they are telling you all week.'

Back in the USA, Buchman was an apparently successful student Christian worker at Pennsylvania State College, so busy he had two phones on his desk. In 1912, Meyer came to the campus where he told Buchman to listen more to God than the phones and to work more personally rather than organising large meetings. Buchman said, 'Since that time, I no longer thought in terms of numbers but in terms of people.'

Buchman developed into a well-known evangelist and personal worker not only in the USA, but all over the world. Another biographer, Gareth Lean, records that Buchman was much influenced by Meyer's books, especially his *Secret of Guidance*. Buchman read it while seeking God's guidance and was especially struck by the words, 'If any man wills to do His will, he shall know.' Later, with the growing rearmament preceding the Second World War, Buchman launched Moral Rearmament, which attempted to change the morality of the social order.

Meyer did not restrict his Keswick ministry to the USA. In 1897, he spoke at the Blackenburg Convention in Germany which had strong similarities with Keswick. In 1903, he returned to Germany and then went to Sweden and Norway with the Keswick message. His Eastern Tour in 1909 of Turkey, Bulgaria, Singapore, China and Japan was under the auspices of the Keswick Convention. In 1923, he fulfilled a long-standing promise to visit

Australia and the mission had the Keswick sounding title of 'For the promotion of Christian living'. A minister who had last heard Meyer thirty years before, when he was a young man attending the YMCA Saturday afternoon meetings, was taken aback by how 'pitifully frail' he looked. He continued, 'Yet everybody was electrified by the vigour with which he spoke.' In Brisbane, aged seventy-six, he spoke on five consecutive days to audiences of over a thousand and 'stirred the hearts and stimulated their love to God and man'. Meyer not only spoke about the Keswick message, his personal power, and reliance upon the strength of the Holy Spirit, embodied it. Probably more than any other Christian, he was the person who took to the world the holiness teaching that emanated from the Keswick tent.

Keswick at Home

It was not just abroad. In the nineteen-twenties, Meyer continued to be one of the main Keswick speakers in Britain. During his lifetime, he addressed twenty-six of the conventions, including five in the period between 1920 and 1929. Other Keswick style gatherings were held in different British destinations and he was a frequent speaker at these.

In earlier chapters, it was explained that Meyer made four major contributions to the development of Keswick. He moved it on from its focus on an individual's personal but insular relationship with God to include practical holiness; that is, how this relationship found expression in the Christian's witness and behaviour in the world. He drew more Nonconformists to Keswick. He supported those who wanted a missionary content at Keswick. He challenged, with some success, the view that social and political activities were not in keeping with the Keswick ethos.

During the nineteen-twenties, the focus on practical holiness continued. Randall commented, 'This is a vital key to understanding Meyer's mass appeal. He believed in worldly holiness.'

Nonconformists continued to attend Keswick, which served as a bridge between them and Anglicans.

The interest in missionary work was maintained. Keswick became a main recruiting ground for evangelical missionary societies.

However, Keswick became divided over social involvement. Some of its followers regarded the war as evidence that pre-war social reforms had not improved humankind. Working class people were disillusioned that the war was followed by low wages or unemployment for many. As Arthur Bryant explains, it led 'to bitterness and strife. There were constant strikes and lock-outs' which inconvenienced the kind of middle class people who attended Christian conventions. In addition, the violent Russian Revolution of 1917 made some fearful of any kind of socialism. The nineteen-twenties saw Labour twice form governments under the leadership of Ramsay MacDonald. In both cases, Labour did not have overall majorities and made few radical innovations but some newspapers wrote alarmingly of the 'red threat'. There was pressure at Keswick for a return to the stance that only conversions could improve society. In 1921, Meyer's friend Frederic Spurr was prepared to re-state the case for Christian social reform but was criticised so strongly that he withdrew. Meyer must have been pleased when Stuart Holden was appointed chair of the Keswick Council in 1923. He was an acceptable Keswick figure, the evangelical vicar of the fashionable St. Paul's in Portman Square in London. Very wealthy, he had an estate in Scotland and a chauffeur driven Rolls Royce. Despite being an Anglican, he had been baptised by Meyer and shared some of his social views. During the miners' strike – which was strongly opposed by most people of wealth – he expressed sympathy for miners.

Yet Holden and others like him were up against a style of fundamentalism which had grown in strength as a reaction to what was called Higher Criticism of the Bible and the fear of creeping theological liberalism even amongst evangelicals. Randall explains that it 'was implacably opposed to a gospel for society, or a social gospel'. Some were also against using any translation of the Bible except the Authorised Version, known as the King James Version. Meyer, incidentally, did draw upon updated versions. The arguments were not all on one side but in 1929 Holden was replaced as chairman, partly because he had spoken on the same platforms as liberal theologians. With Holden gone, Keswick was again characterised by a suspicion of social welfare and politics.

Meyer continued to encourage Christians to be socially involved, which was to be expressed at three levels. One was practical help to individuals. He listed examples like, 'Helping perplexed and laden fellow-travellers; women helping tired mothers with troublesome children; sheltering young girls; inviting young men and women to our homes, who are strangers in London; noticing the hungry little faces that gaze into bakers' shops, and giving them wholesome food.' Next was participation in Christian and other charitable agencies which helped those in social need. This would include church based organisations like those which had flourished at Melbourne Hall and Christ Church and also national Christian bodies. Meyer was a supporter of both Dr. Barnardo's and the National Children's Home and Orphanage. Lastly, political pressure and action. In the nineteen-twenties, Meyer still linked the values of the Labour Party to the teachings of Jesus. Few at Keswick would have agreed.

Despite his views, Meyer continued as a major figure at Keswick. After all, he was a world-wide Keswick speaker, was accepted as one of the leading Nonconformist spokespersons, and he had good relationships with numbers of Anglicans, including bishops and archbishops. Yet he did not push his social reform view stance too strongly at Keswick in these years. Perhaps he knew the odds were now against him, perhaps he felt too old for conflict, or perhaps it was that he wanted to concentrate on another matter – revival.

Meyer longed for revival, a great outpouring of the Holy Spirit upon the nation. As early as 1898 he had written that evangelistic work amongst the unsaved was not sufficient, 'We need more a revival in the Church. ... Revive the Church and you must touch the world.' He sought out revivals and witnessed small scale ones in the USA. As explained, he was present at parts of the Welsh Revival of 1904 to 1905. Meyer sometimes spoke about a new Pentecost. He does not seem to have personally experienced speaking in tongues and the ministry of healing but he was not nervous about these manifestations which were present in the book of Acts. Some Keswick leaders were worried about 'excesses', disliked the reference to Pentecost as a description of revival, and did not embrace the Welsh revival.

The Keswick Council, however, could not ignore the subject when, in 1921, a local revival stemmed from a Keswick meeting. It had been organised in Lowestoft by an Anglican and a Baptist minister with the speaker being the Revd Douglas Brown, a London Baptist minister. Hundreds of people were converted and it spread into other parts of East Anglia. The Lowestoft ministers spoke about it at the Keswick of 1921. The Council asked Meyer and three others to suggest a way forward and responded to their suggestion to invite Brown to lead the Bible Readings in 1922. Maurice Rowlandson, who later became the secretary of the Keswick Convention, wrote that the response to Brown's talk was so great that 'Pied-Piper like he led enquirers down to the Drill Hall in the town' while Meyer stayed in the tent to conduct an impromptu meeting for others. Rowlandson reckons that up to three thousand people 'stepped forward significantly in their Christian lives that day'. The impact and interest were short-lived. Meyer must have been disappointed but remained expectant. He believed that revival could well start in India, China or Korea. Today it appears that his hopes may well have been fulfilled.

Missionary Enthusiasm

As a boy, Meyer frequently heard about missionaries and says he was stirred by heroes such as David Livingstone and Robert Moffatt. He commented, 'So profound was my veneration for them that it never entered my head that I should be a missionary. That I might become a Christian minister was within the limits of possibility, but to be a missionary – *never*.'

As a minister, his concern for missionary work quickened at Melbourne Hall in Leicester. He brought missionary speakers to the church and was personally challenged by the Cambridge Seven when they set out for China. He organised missionary conferences and numbers of local young people volunteered to go abroad.

At his first pastorate at Regent's Park, Meyer continued to have a missionary focus. In 1891, a young man started attending Regent's Park Chapel when he moved to London. He went to the cheap teas on Sunday afternoons for those in lodgings and Meyer welcomed him. Soon he drew him into a band of young Christians who visited 'doss houses' and other places of need. From this small band, at least seven men eventually went to the mission field. It was during a sermon preached by Meyer that this young man heard the call. He became the Revd E. Palgrave Davy of South India. Afterwards, they kept in touch, Meyer sent him books, and they met up when Davy came home on furloughs.

Cecil Robertson became a Christian under Meyer's ministry at Christ Church but later worshipped at Regent's Park with his parents. He became an outstanding doctor and chose to go to China with the Baptist Missionary Society. In 1909, Meyer, who had just returned to Regent's Park, conducted the last service that Robertson attended there. In China, Robertson used his medical skills during times of violence and revolution, serving both missionaries and Chinese wounded. Soon after, he died of typhus in 1913 at the age of twenty-eight. Meyer was very moved and, with the family's co-operation, wrote a book *Cecil Robertson of Sianfu*, which depicts the tremendous impact he made on Chinese people; indeed the Chinese government decorated him 'for services to the state' after his death, a remarkable honour at a time of frequent hostility to foreigners. Meyer concluded, 'In all the earth there is no profession more noble, more interesting, more valuable to our human kind, or more pleasing to the Redeemer than that to which Cecil Robertson gave himself.'

During his first spell at Christ Church, Meyer gave frequent updates about Christ Church's missionaries in the church magazine. For instance, in 1898, he listed five men and four women serving abroad and three more in training. The Christ Church Jubilee Year Book of 1926 gives details of serving missionaries, some of whom first went out during Meyer's ministries. They included the following. Mr. and Mrs John Harris who survived the atrocities in the Congo and brought back photographic evidence to place before the government. Dr. Florence Payne went to India where her own health broke down, being the only doctor in a large area. After recovery in Britain, she eventually went to serve in Jerusalem. The Revd Wilson and Mrs Geller went to China in 1897 and in 1926 were still there. So too were the Revd Charles and Mrs Fairclough.

It is impossible to enumerate all those who became missionaries under Meyer's ministries, no more than those who responded to his missionary appeals at Keswick. All that can be said is that they were many.

As well as delivering the call to missionaries, Meyer also identified with a number of missionary societies. Fullerton stated that the Baptist Missionary Society 'was his first love' but he gave more time to non-denominational ones like the China Inland Mission, the London Missionary Society and, in particular, to the Regions Beyond Missionary Union (R.B.M.U.). His concern for mission abroad was recognised and intensified when, in 1895, he became associate editor of *The Missionary Review*, which was edited by his friend, the American the Revd A. T. Pierson. As mentioned, while at Christ Church, Meyer also founded a small missionary training college which later merged with one run by the R.B.M.U.

In the late 1890s, Meyer wrote in *The Life of Faith* that he felt God was entrusting him to be a messenger to missionaries and during his trips he made a special point of talking with them in India, South Africa and the Far East. Fullerton gives attention to a trip he made to Syria in 1901 where he visited schools and a hospital run by the Friends (or Quakers). He used their premises, along with tents supplied by Thomas Cook & Son (Cook was a strong Baptist), as a base for a conference which drew over two hundred missionaries from many miles away. He then addressed the Syrian Protestant College and its five hundred students.

During his tours, Meyer realised that he longed to be a missionary himself. During his Far East trip of 1909, he wrote, 'As I look into the faces of these Chinese my heart loves them. ... I long to get to them with the message of Christ.. Too late in life I learn what I have missed in not being a missionary. It is a great and profound *miss*, that in my case can not be undone.' In Singapore, he frequently saw the many men who pulled rickshaws, which may have reminded him of some of the cab drivers who attended the Brotherhood at Christ Church, for he penned, 'If only I were not too old, I would like to start a great Brotherhood movement amongst these 18,000 men ... the fields are white, but the reapers are few.'

It came to a head when Meyer, in 1920, was staying with friends at Skelmorlie on the Clyde coast in Scotland. Two of Livingstone's African followers, who had accompanied his body home, had built there a wooden hut of the kind in which Livingstone died. Kneeling alone in the hut, Meyer rededicated his remaining years to the Lord for the furtherance of the gospel abroad. He must be one of the few people whose missionary zeal increased with age.

It was his fifth turning point and it seemed to invigorate him. Soon after, the R.B.M.U. was in a financial and administrative crisis. Despite being in his seventies, Meyer stepped into the breach as Acting Director and General Secretary in order to promote its work in the Congo and India. He went to the office several days a week, directing affairs, speaking at meetings all over the country, attending the annual conference at Bournemouth and keeping in touch with its home for missionaries' children. He organised the office and improved the finances. When he stepped back to become Director Emeritus the year before he died, it still needed £3000. Significantly in his will, Meyer left the bulk of his money to the R.B.M.U. (which received £4,000) and to a children's home, of which more will be said.

The R.B.M.U. was a traditional kind of missionary society which sent British missionaries to convert the heathen. Meyer backed this approach but he also thought and wrote deeply about missionary strategy. More than once he wrote words like. 'The best work our missionaries are doing is that of training and educating the native Christians who will carry the Gospel to their fellow-countrymen.' He foresaw that missionaries would be forced out of some countries and that indigenous Christians would take over the leadership. This became a commonplace view but was a radical one in his time. Further, he stated that if Christianity declined in the west, eventually missionaries from the east would evangelise it. As he put it, 'The East would a second time give to the West the Pearl of immeasurable price.'

In 1919, Meyer wrote in his book on Peter that Confucius, Buddha and Mohammed had 'no medicine for the soul. There is no satisfaction but in Christ.' This was the traditional view of Christian missionaries. Yet, in his trips, Meyer met and was impressed by spiritual non-Christians of other faiths. He struggled with this and in April 1928, he wrote in *The Sunday Express*, 'And may there not have been myriads, in all lands and ages, who have been true to such light as they had, following the gleam – and will not these come from the east and west, from north and south, as Christ said, and sit down in the Kingdom of God.' Meyer was not departing from his evangelical beliefs for in the same article he upheld the divinity of Christ and the necessity of his incarnation, death and resurrection. But he did respect sincere followers of other faiths and was content to leave them to the mercy and justice of a loving God.

Adventism
In that same national newspaper article in 1928, Meyer proclaimed, 'The intrusion of God, in the Person of Christ, into our nature and world, leads me to expect a second Advent, when his love will again be manifested in His overcoming and perfected victory. Death and Hades are doomed.'

Adventism gripped Meyer during the last decade of his life but it interested him well before the nineteen-twenties. In 1905, some of London's newspapers took notice of his view that during the first century some Christians had been swept up into heaven as a kind of forerunner of what would happen. Meyer retained a leaflet which advertised his preaching a series of second advent sermons during the war, with titles such as, 'The Apostate Church and the Real Church', 'The Turk and his Doom', and 'The Jew Must Come to his Own'.

It was the war which stimulated interest in Adventism among a number of evangelicals. They saw it as signifying mankind's failure to build a better world so that any hope must rest on the second coming of Christ alone. Further, in 1917, the British government revealed that it was prepared to allow the Jewish people to return to their original homeland in Palestine. Adventists saw this as a confirmation of a prophecy in the Bible that such an event would happen just before the second coming of Christ.

Following the government's announcement, Meyer played a leading part in drawing together Christian leaders who, like himself, were looking for God's intervention into the world. They included William Fullerton, Stuart Holden, the Preb. Webb-Peploe and Dr. Campbell Morgan. They formed the Advent Testimony Movement (A.T.M.) with Meyer as president. Its beliefs included the coming of Christ at any moment, that the church would then be taken to be with the Lord, and that Jewish people would be restored to their own land and converted by Christ. Another leaflet of the time advertised a three day conference in May 1920 to be held at Christ Church, under the auspices of the A.T.M., on the subject 'The Holy Spirit in Relation to the Church: the Nation: the World'. The movement attracted large crowds at its meetings, gained the support of some Keswick speakers and published a monthly paper.

A surprising addition to the Adventist cause came in the person of Christabel Pankhurst, the former suffragette leader. One of her ambitions had been fulfilled in 1918 when a limited number of women did receive the vote, but her move to Adventism had less to do with completing this feminist battle and more to a religious conversion. This was not the classic evangelical conversion of a sinner coming to Jesus but rather a conviction that the coming of Christ was foretold in the Bible and that Christ was the only hope of the world.

She had heard Meyer preach in 1921 just before she went to the USA and Canada. On her return, she sought him out and, as Timothy Larsen explains in his study of Christabel Pankhurst, this proved a wise choice because Meyer was 'the most prominent and respected English conservative evangelical minister of the day'. Meyer took her under his wing and opened the doors to speaking engagements. Meyer had been sympathetic towards the votes for women campaign and had no qualms about Christabel's ministry. As a director of the publishers Morgan & Scott, he had an outlet for her writings and he wrote a forward for two of her books. One, *The Lord Cometh: The World Crisis Explained* (1923), achieved very large sales. She developed a high regard for Meyer and wrote of 'his wonderful serenity and glowing saintliness, his intense concentration on his Master's service, his selfless interest in the efforts of others'.

Thus Meyer boosted the movement both by his own preaching and by his ability to draw others into it. Another strength rested in his refusal to claim to be a scholarly academic and so he rarely delved into the minutiae of Adventism. As Randall carefully explains, there were different views about the timing and nature of Christ's return. It was enough for Meyer that Christ was coming and coming soon. His straightforward views, his refusal to join in the fierce battles between different types of Adventists, along with his personal authority and friendliness, enabled him to hold a disparate body together.

Randall pinpoints another contribution by Meyer. Although he travelled to the USA to meet other Adventists, he was careful not to identify with the rigid fundamentalism of many there. As mentioned, the fundamentalists were also making their presence felt at Keswick. It thrived on opposition to other Christians whom they regarded as theologically suspect. Meyer wanted British Adventists to be less negative and more positive, to put less emphasis on in-fighting and more on the outward spreading of the message of the second coming. As Randall aptly concluded,

'Meyer was not prepared to dig a Fundamentalist bunker from which to wage war against other Christian leaders.'

For Meyer, Adventism had three great benefits. It was a spur to holiness. He could preach at Keswick that Christians needed to be more holy in the expectation of the appearance of Christ. Further, it drew Christians of different denominations together. The extent of the A.T.M. must not be exaggerated. The majority of church leaders and churches were not involved with it while its membership never exceeded two and a half thousand. None the less, when Meyer saw hundreds of Christians casting denominational loyalty aside and coming together to welcome Christ, he felt he was seeing the church as it should be. Not least, Adventism was a personal boost. Meyer was always seeking new spiritual experiences and the expectancy of Christ's return seemed to re-charge him. Indeed, Christabel Pankhurst observed that in the last year of his life 'he gained very definitely in power and spiritual insight'.

Meyer the Pessimist?

After the war, Meyer gave much time to Adventism. Did this mean that he shared the pessimism about evangelism, a rejection of social involvement, and a belief that the world was doomed which was found in some of its followers? Ian Randall gives some – but only some – support to this view and writes, 'Meyer was, in his later years, part of a process of retreat from the world and of narrowing theological horizons which was evident in British evangelicalism.' He adds that part of this may have come from a sense of failure that evangelism had not reached the masses. He states, 'But after the war a more pessimistic expectation of human affairs generally, tempered only by his confidence in the work of the Spirit, especially in nurturing a surviving remnant, made his ministry more pietist and less concerned with institutional change.'

Certainly Meyer the Adventist did sometimes make statements to support these views. In an approving introduction to Christabel Pankhurst's book of 1923, he indicated a lack of faith in political or social contributions to social well-being. However, as Randall himself cautioned, Meyer's remarks were 'probably designed to resonate with Pankhurst's polemic'. His position must be seen in the context of all of his activities in the nineteen-twenties.

Did he regard evangelism as a failure? Soon after the war, Meyer might have been interpreted as disillusioned that the church was not advancing. He wrote in his book on Peter, 'Suicide is said to be on the increase. Immorality and the laxity of the marriage tie suggest the wane of love, and hope, and faith.' But turn the page and he is not in despair but is calling for the proclamation of Christ, that is, for evangelism. As late as 1927, he wrote the forward to the biography of his friend John Wilson of Woolwich, who had been pastor in the same church since 1877 and built up a large number of social agencies and won many converts. Meyer observed that Woolwich was losing families as they moved to the suburbs. But, instead of despair, Meyer saw this as an opportunity for evangelism to draw in the working classes, 'who are not opposed to the Gospel of Christ.'

In addition, Meyer regarded the second coming not just as something to be waited for but also as an evangelistic spur to the unconverted to turn to Christ before it was too late. Not least, in terms of work and effort, Meyer gave much of his time to missionary societies which, if nothing else, were vehicles for evangelism. His faith in evangelism remained unabated.

It is true that Meyer was less outspoken about political issues in the nineteen-twenties. This did not mean he considered his political activities a failure. The campaign over the Education Act fizzled out. However, Frank Prochaska explains that although the voluntary church schools did receive statutory grants, the higher standards expected of them 'exacerbated their long-standing financial problems' and their number eventually declined. There was evidence, too, that problems of heavy drinking did fall while the purity movement, under the leadership of Josephine Butler, who died in 1906, had some notable successes. It was rather that Meyer now lacked a political role and platform. He was not the president of the Baptist Union and did not have political responsibilities within the Free Church Council. Moreover, the Liberal Party, which had been the mouthpiece for many Nonconformists, had lost ground dramatically. Asquith and Lloyd George led rival factions and in 1916 the latter made alliances with the Conservatives. Meyer was still loyal to Asquith and Shakespeare to Lloyd George while the influential Revd John Clifford moved towards the Labour Party. In the general election of 1922, the Liberal vote collapsed and Labour became the main opposition. Even if he had wanted it, Meyer no longer had a political voice.

This did not mean that Meyer lost faith in politics. He still saw a connection between the aims and values of the Labour Party and the teachings of Jesus. He did not side with those at Keswick who rejected the social gospel.

Nor did Meyer turn against the social-change role of church and Christian agencies. If he had done so he would have regretted much of his work at Melbourne Hall and Christ Church. On the contrary, he continued to look back to it with some pride, almost as a golden era. The difference was that Meyer was now too old to undertake this physically demanding work himself. However, during this period, as will be shown, he did found and actively support a children's home. Although Randall argues that during this period Meyer was in partial retreat from the world, he also acknowledges that he 'never repudiated his social vision'.

In an article purporting to be a letter 'To one who is growing old', Meyer wrote, 'Don't be always dwelling on the good old times.' He argued that the former times were often the bad old times characterised by the press gang and appalling conditions in factories and that there was 'more light' in the present. He continued, 'Dare to believe that the Angel who led your generation will lead the next.' Some pessimist!

Even in his younger days, Meyer, like many Christians, was a mixture of pessimist and optimist. In 1904, a perceptive journalist, Raymond Blathwayt, commented on Meyer's pessimistic identification of the immorality and indifference to religion of much of the population. Simultaneously, he wrote that

Meyer was also 'a convinced optimist, ever seeing the bright side of everything, ever hopeful, ever vigorous, ever confident of the ultimate triumph of good over evil'. In short, Meyer recognised the capacity for good and bad in all people and accepted a two-fold mission to help build the kind of social conditions which encouraged good behaviour and to offer the Christ who could rescue people from sin.

Meyer did not become more pessimistic with old age. In 1927, he published an article on 'Thoughts at 80.' His first words were 'On my eightieth birthday I must confess myself a confirmed optimist. ... I am well aware of the insidious evils which are working in the dark against the well-being of society, but they do not sap my faith that mankind will win through at last.' He then listed signs of better things such as 'proposals afoot for a better understanding between capital and labour, or the creation of the League of Nations, or the substitution of thousands of working men's dwellings for the over-crowded slums. Surely these are preparing for and heralding a new wave of advance.' Above all, he saw the coming of a new heaven on earth with the arrival of Christ, although he could not tell if it would come instantly or by a protracted process. His only regret was the 'advance of these thievish years, that steal away my chance of sharing in and speeding the next decades of progress'.

The Homeless Children's Aid and Adoption Society
In his seventies, Meyer showed his continuing belief in human institutions by establishing a children's home. In post-war Britain, he became more concerned about the plight of unmarried mothers and their children. The numbers of illegitimate births were rising but enormous stigma still attached to both the mothers and their children. It was financially difficult for the mothers to keep their children yet complicated to find a reliable foster home or to arrange adoption. Indeed, the first Adoption Act was not passed until 1926. Meyer and some friends, particularly a Mrs Caroline Mary Haymes, a member of Christ Church, had helped individuals but decided more was required. In 1920,

they formed an organisation under the unwieldy title of The Homeless Children's Aid and Adoption Society, with the aim of accommodating children until suitable substitute parents could be found. This was followed by a Children's Home to take in the children (called Meyer's Children's Home) at Hutchison House in Leytonstone which took up to thirty small children before they were adopted, fostered or until the mother could cope. It was a voluntary home and so the committee was responsible for raising the funds.

A press cutting of 1926 reports on the annual meeting of the society with Meyer in the chair. It told of a small baby, about four weeks old, left outside the society's office with a note saying that the mother was too ill to look after him and asking that he be adopted. The police were informed and notices put in the press but she could not be traced. The society gave him the name of Frederick (after Meyer), Poole (after Meyer's successor at Christ Church, who was also on the committee), Hawkstone (after Hawkstone Hall). Later he was relieved of this cumbersome name when placed with adoptive parents and taking their name.

The organisation lasted long after Meyer. In 1939, the home was evacuated and re-opened after the war as a Mother and Baby Home where mothers came to have their babies and to make decisions about the future. In all, nearly seven thousand children were placed for adoption. In 1980, it merged with the Mission of Hope and finally closed in 1992.

The Last Years
Meyer did not put his feet up in his last years. As well as still travelling abroad, in Britain he was preaching at Keswick, advent meetings and other engagements. All this on top of his oversight of his beloved R.B.M.U.

July 1926 was a momentous year for him. It marked the one hundred and fiftieth anniversary of the American Declaration of Independence and the newspapers contained reports on Christ Church's links with the USA, which had resulted in the building of the Lincoln Tower. It was also fifty years since the congregation of Surrey Chapel left to start at Christ Church and Meyer kept the programme which showed the celebrations spread over three days of the 4th to the 6th of July. On the Sunday morning, Meyer preached in the same pulpit on the same date on the same text – 'Christ is all in all' – as Dr. Newman Hall fifty years before. Further meetings and recitals continued and culminated on the Tuesday with a public meeting at The Ring, the original Surrey Chapel which had become a boxing stadium. The speakers clambered into the boxing ring where Meyer amused the packed audience by pretending to spar with the main speaker, the Revd Dinsdale Young. The celebrations caught the attention of the press and Meyer's papers contain over seventy cuttings of the events.

In the same month, Meyer was present at the Seventh World Congress of Christian Endeavour at Queen's Hall, London where two thousand delegates from nearly thirty countries listened to David Lloyd George and Ramsay MacDonald amongst the many speakers. Meyer had long supported this movement, which he admired for its nurturing and training of young Christians.

Another celebration came on 8 April 1927, Meyer's eightieth birthday. The pulpit was strewn with flowers, he cut a huge cake made in the shape of the Lincoln Tower and received a number of gifts, including a portable radio. When presented with a cheque for £800, Meyer assured the congregation that it would go to causes dear to his heart, especially the children's home. In a general letter of thanks, Meyer wrote, still with his beautifully clear handwriting, that he could not reply individually to the mass of letters and cards and stated, 'I can only lay these wreaths at the feet of our dear Master Christ.'

Soon after, he left for the USA and Canada where he travelled fifteen thousand miles over three months and spoke at between two to four meetings most days.

In July 1928 he spoke for the last time at Keswick. A photograph of the speakers reveals him looking small, almost shrivelled, beside the others. But his preaching was still powerful. His last talk at a convention was one on his familiar territory of 'deepening of spiritual life'. Held at Brighton in October 1928, he gave the closing address for more than an hour to over a thousand listeners.

In January 1929, his wife, Jeannie, died at Bournemouth. Meyer conducted the service at the graveside and said, 'Farewell, dear one to the body, but not to the soul.' Two days later, he insisted on keeping an engagement to preach in Bromley. He spoke on, 'Yea, though I walk through the valley of the shadow of death, I will fear no evil' but did not refer to his own loss.

His last speaking engagement, where he preached twice, was at the Wesley Chapel in London. He thus gave his final sermon a few yards from John Wesley's burial place. They were both men who kept on preaching well into their eighties.

A few days later, Mrs Caroline Hames, who had become Meyer's secretary, accompanied him to a nursing home in Streatham. A bronchial attack followed by heart weakness caused him to cancel a proposed trip to America. Instead he entered a nursing home in Boscombe. He knew he was dying yet dictated an article he had promised for the press and over thirty letters of farewell. One was to the officers and members of Christ Church. It must have given him some pleasure to recall that 'The majority of the officers were young men in my first pastorate (at Christ Church).' His daughter, Mrs Hilda Tatam, Sister Margaret and his secretary were constantly with him. His elder sister, granddaughters, and a number of friends came to visit him. He died on 28th March 1929.

The funeral took place at Christ Church where the streets were thronged with local people to pay their respects. The service, in the packed church, ended, at Meyer's request, with the Hallelujah Chorus.

The newspapers were full of the news of his death along with glowing obituaries. Tributes flowed in from all over the world. His friend William Fullerton wrote movingly, 'Other men have lived as long: other men have travelled as far: other men have preached as often: other men have been loved as much: but none have combined all of these as fully as he.' In a sense, Meyer lived many lives but, as he put it a few months before his death, 'If I had a hundred lives, they should be at Christ's disposal.'

9

F. B. MEYER: AN ASSESSMENT

'The two talents'

Frederick Brotherton Meyer was not alone in being a prominent Christian minister. In Victorian times, despite the growth of secularism, criticisms about the historical accuracy of the Bible and the rise of Darwinism, some churchmen remained household names. Archbishops of Canterbury like Benson and Temple were powerful figures, Cardinal Newman (as he became) caused a major controversy when he moved from the Anglican to the Roman Catholic Church, while Cardinal Manning was a recognised social as well as religious leader. General William Booth was famous for creating the Salvation Army and David Livingstone was a Boys' Own hero for his exploits in Africa. Even at the start of the twentieth century, Sir Robert Ensor wrote, 'Preachers of any merit still drew large and attentive audiences, and a considerable number had what might be termed national reputations.'

Meyer did have a national reputation within the Nonconformist world. However, he was just one of a number of leading preachers. A. C. Underwood in his *A History of the English Baptists*, first published in 1947, rated Charles Haddon Spurgeon, John Clifford and Alexander Maclaren as the three greatest Baptist ministers of the Victorian era. Spurgeon was a conservative evangelical who regularly preached to over five thousand at the Metropolitan Tabernacle. His published sermons ran to sixty-three volumes and he initiated a number of social agencies, including a large children's home. John Clifford was a more liberal evangelical who spent nearly all his ministerial years in one church. Twice president of the Baptist Union, he had strong socialist leanings, was a member of the Fabian Society and was known as 'the uncrowned king of militant Nonconformity'. Alexander Maclaren was not noted as a pastoral worker but was considered a preacher without peer.

Underwood gives Meyer a mere two pages, perhaps because, unlike the others, he did not confine himself to the Baptist denomination. But it is not the intention of this chapter to rank Meyer in the ministerial league – he would have loathed that. It is sufficient to say that he was a great minister and one who is now overlooked. This chapter will attempt to identify his strengths and achievements and to spell out some of his personal characteristics.

The Two Talents

Meyer sometimes said that the inscription on his grave should be the Biblical verse from the parable of the talents, 'Then he that had two talents came.' He was saying that he had just two talents – preaching and writing.

Meyer must have been a wonderful preacher. Not only did he draw vast crowds but he kept their attention. He was constantly in demand in Britain and in many other parts of the world. Indeed, Randall says that in the early part of the twentieth century, he was 'Britain's foremost international preacher'. He seemed to hold audiences in the palm of his hand. His more formal speeches, like his presidential address to the Baptist Union, could spark off cheering from normally sedate Baptists. Yet Meyer was quick to point out that beautiful sermons were useless unless they made a spiritual impact on men and women. And that frequently happened. At Keswick one year, he spoke on the need to put things right in our lives before approaching God. The next day the post office ran out of money orders as people repaid others they had swindled, deceived or failed to repay. Later at Keswick, his missionary address led to many coming forward to commit themselves to service. And not just in Britain. His talks on his overseas tours led to what now would be called 'rave reviews'.

Just as impressive was the effect of his preaching at Melbourne Hall and Christ Church where hundreds were converted, took the pledge against drink, and committed themselves to holy living. Too numerous to report are the instances he gives of individuals who approached him after a service who wanted to seek forgiveness, who wanted help with a deep sin, who wanted to come back to God after years of drift.

With much written in praise of Meyer's preaching, it is almost a relief to learn that sometimes his standards did slip. John Pollock, in his history of Keswick, says that sometimes the quality of his talks was affected adversely by his constant travels; meaning, apparently, his hurried preparations on trains. On the other hand, he also says that Meyer 'delivered some of the greatest addresses ever heard there'.

What was it that made him such an effective speaker? As Jennie Street frankly concedes, it was not his looks or physical presence, 'His personal appearance is not imposing; on the contrary, some find their first sight of his slight figure and somewhat worn-looking face rather disappointing.' He did not have a dramatic style in the pulpit and did not walk up and down or shout. In the USA, journalists, drawn by his reputation, probably expected another Moody and were puzzled as to just how he held the congregation. As one wrote, 'His sermons are a conversation in which he does all the talking – nothing more.'

Several factors contributed to his effectiveness. Although he never shouted and did not have a microphone, he possessed a clear voice with well-articulated words which reached to all corners. The content of his talks tended to be easily understood and threw light on everyday Christianity. A number of his talks were published and one, probably aimed at young people, was called 'The "Must" of Sacrifice'. Its outline, which was typical of his approach, was as follows.

First, an early sentence to catch attention. In this talk it was, 'Self-sacrifice is rightly recognised as the supreme trait of a noble character.'

Second, an example or illustration from secular life. Here he outlined Abraham Lincoln's reluctance to leave his home town to take the dangerous task of President of the USA, which eventually led to his murder. An example of self-sacrifice. Sometimes he would take his examples from science, in which he was surprisingly well read, or the wonders of nature.

Third, an emphasis on Jesus and his self-sacrifice. Meyer was a Christ-centred preacher and his words about his Lord would touch deep emotions.

Fourth, application. He proclaimed, 'Looking at this stupendous act, shall we not catch the infection of His self-giving? Shall we not follow Him so far as we can?'

Fifth, examples of the kind of sacrifices which his listeners might have to make.

Meyer's notes for a talk made up less than a page. Yet he took time to memorise its shape and, when he spoke, it flowed with one sentence following another in logical order.

Meyer never claimed to be a theologian, indeed he said, 'My theology, I fear, has been left hopelessly out of account.' Maybe, but he had a deep interest in what was called biblical archaeology and in a book, *The Art of Life*, he argued that contemporary studies were confirming the historical accuracy of the Scriptures. In the same book, he showed that he did read modern higher criticism. He dismissed those who dwelt on the apparent cruel punishments and bloody wars of the Old Testament by arguing that 'the Bible is the Record and History of a Progressive Revelation [his capitals] ... and that in Jesus Christ is the only perfect revelation of God'. He was prepared to bring this approach into his sermons so that his preaching was both rooted in historical facts while being open to modern discoveries and interpretations. In short, he was relevant.

Of course, his talks were not always to the same kind of audience. A lecture to learned ministers was different to that with working class women. Another of Meyer's strengths was his ability to adapt to different kinds of listeners. At conventions, his manner was serious, almost intense. Yet even here there was a difference between his talks which focussed on a theme – like how to walk more closely with God – and those which concentrated on a Biblical character. In the latter, he had the knack of almost living alongside Moses or Peter or Jesus as he went into great detail about their lives. Yet every now and then he applied their example to the present day activities of Christians.

By contrast to a convention of Christians in a large tent, he also spoke to non-Christians in the open air. Climbing on a chair, he would use something at hand as his way of connecting with the crowds – telegraph poles to illustrate prayer, the crescent moon to show the incompleteness of life without Christ, water pipes as the starting point to a short talk about the living waters of Christ and so on. All mixed with *bonhomie* and a quick wit ready to respond to hecklers.

Despite his middle class and conventional upbringing, Meyer learned to communicate with working class audiences. He had a relaxed and breezy manner which went down well. He deliberately sought smiles and laughter when talking with local women. One journalist, who accompanied Meyer, recorded in 1909, 'I do not think I have ever had heartier laughs than when in the company of Mr. Meyer.' Yet he did not undermine his serious message and many were the men in the Brotherhood and women in the Women's at Home who responded to his messages.

Successful preaching is not just about good techniques and well-written talks. Meyer had something extra. Power. An article in a New York paper in 1899 commented on one of his sermons, 'There was no attempt at oratory, no effort to produce great thoughts ... yet one felt that there was a power in the message.' Other observers also contrasted the quietness of his approach with the strength of its effect. Meyer often preached about the power of the Holy Spirit and his speaking was an example of it in action.

If preaching was one talent, the other was writing. He was a prolific writer who published over a hundred books, booklets and pamphlets. Many were translated into German and Swedish and several into Hindi, Singalese, Burmese, Chinese, Greek and Syrian. In all, an estimated five million copies of his books have been published. In addition, he edited a number of magazines and wrote countless articles. He had a close connection with *The Christian* and for some time wrote two pages a week for it.

His writing days appeared to start at Melbourne Hall with a series of small booklets. Later he wrote longer books but also of the size which could be slipped into a pocket. I have one in front of me now called *The Future Tenses of the Blessed Life*, published in 1894 which consists of 154 pages but whose cover is a mere five inches by three and a half.

His longer and larger books were of six main kinds. Biographies of Biblical characters like Abraham, Joseph, David, John the Baptist and Paul. Expository books such as *Christ in Isaiah* and *From the Pit to the Throne*. Books based on his sermons like *Blessed Are Ye, Talks on the Beatitudes* and *Five 'Musts' of the Christian Life*. Volumes on aspects of Christian Living or how to live the Christian life like *The Art of Living* and *The Directory of the Devout Life*. Books of daily readings including *Through the Bible Day by Day* and *Daily Bible Readings*. Lastly, three books about his own life and travels, *The Bells of Is* (about his time in Leicester), *Reveries and Realities* (about his ministry at Christ Church), and *A Winter in South Africa*.

Clearly Meyer's books were widely read and appreciated. Street wrote, 'Never a day passes but he receives letters from people who have been helped by his writings.' Fullerton was not sure about the impact on future generations and thought that Meyer 'touched so many subjects that perhaps his message to his own times will scarcely appeal to the future'. In fact, a number of his devotional books are still being re-printed.

Why were his books so successful? A clue is found in the preface to two of his books. In one he said that their purpose was to 'most readily help Christian people in the varied circumstances of daily life'. He wanted to promote holiness or sanctification. In another, he warned 'There is too much of mere sentiment and emotion in what goes by the name of religion and too little practical living.'

It was this combination of spirituality as expressed in everyday living that made his books relevant to readers.

Certainly Meyer advocated prayer and daily reflection on the Bible. He urged Christians to keep in fellowship with other Christians and to worship regularly. He also dwelt on their relationships with other people and with their possessions. This approach can be seen in the following small selection of his topics: turning the other cheek when harmed by others; how to love Christians you don't like; showing kindness to neighbours and strangers; what to do when worn down by care and anxiety. He gave particular attention to the Christian's attitude to money. While earning money is a legitimate even essential activity, he warns believers about the dangers of hoarding it. His advice to business people was to retain enough for the maintenance of their families, to put aside some for the development of the business, to keep some for old age 'but when all this is done, look upon the remainder as God's to be used for Him'. He gave some examples about people he knew. One had the very large income of £8,000 a year but lived on £250 and gave away the remainder. Another, a governess, earned £100 a year and gave away £50. He wrote, 'Let us not hoard what we have got. ... Let us be prodigal and spendthrift of our wealth.'

Meyer also regarded healthy living as a Christian duty. He advised Christians to take healthy exercise and to participate in sport. As to diet, he recommended 'plenty of wholemeal bread, porridge or Quaker oats, shredded wheat or grape-nuts ... don't smoke; don't drink alcohol.' His argument was that God gave us bodies which should be looked after and would thus be more fit for His service.

Not least, it must be said that Meyer was a straightforward and skilled writer. He read but rarely quoted from learned commentators as they would bore readers. Instead, he attempted 'to state my own conclusions as simply and clearly as possible'. His writings, like his talks, are full of similes, metaphors, examples and illustrations drawn from life. Having been mountain climbing, he explained that no microbes of corruption and disease could live in the air of the high Alps and in like manner no sin would survive if Christians moved in the pure atmosphere of God. He explained that a wonderful fountain in Rome disappeared for centuries because it had been choked by rubbish. Finally the rubbish was removed and the fountain was useful again. Similarly, Christians have to throw out the rubbish and evil which chokes their goodness and usefulness.

Often simple and straightforward, there were times when the literary muse seemed to come upon Meyer. His imagination enabled him to bring Biblical scenes to life. He could wax lyrical about the countryside and birds. Interestingly, Meyer was angered by the killing of wildlife which he regarded as an essential part of God's creation. He condemned those who wore as ornaments the plumage of sea-birds, 'the taking of which involves whole nests of young ones in a tedious death'. And not just the country. He loved what he called 'The poetry of London streets'. In these styles, Meyer draws readers into the beauty of the earth which, he argued, was evidence of a planned creation by Almighty God.

But taste and see. In writing this study, I have read a number of Meyer's books. Most were written over a hundred years ago and I had anticipated tomes in lengthy Victorian prose of immediate interest only to people who were still Victorians at heart. In fact, I have often been gripped by them. I have found that they dealt with some of the difficulties I faced. I have often been strengthened by his words and sometimes inspired by them. I understand why they are still in print.

The Church Builder

Meyer had far more than two talents and he had multiple achievements. A preacher and writer, who drew many people to God and inspired others to understand the work and readiness of the Holy Spirit to enhance their Christian lives. A Baptist leader, who raised enormous amounts of money and set out a strategy to train and support ministers. A Nonconformist statesman, who drew disparate denominations together, who strove for their distinctive beliefs while maintaining personal friendships with members of other denominations with whom he disagreed, and who led from the front in political battles. A campaigner for civic righteousness. A president of a number of national Christian societies, he was sometimes called President Meyer. At various times, he was president of the National Union of Christian Endeavour, the National Sunday School Association (or Union), the Young Christians' Missionary Union, as well as the Baptist Union and the Free Church Council and others. He took his duties seriously, chairing meetings, planning strategies, speaking at rallies and sometimes travelling abroad on their behalf. Not least, he was zealous for missionary work in which he recruited volunteers, taught them at colleges, visited them in their outposts and, in his eighties, took over the administration of a missionary society which lacked leadership and money. And much more. Here I limit myself to two of the most outstanding achievements, his capacity as a church builder and his outstanding role as a social activist.

He was a church minister for fifty years. In Leicester, Meyer and his supporters did erect a new church of bricks and mortar. But he was a great church builder in the sense of drawing people in to worship, to be converted, to be strengthened in their Christian lives. He did this in a small way in Liverpool. At Priory Road Baptist Chapel in York, he baptised a modest number of believers and then met with the evangelist Dwight Moody whose enthusiasm and commitment he took on board. At Victoria Road Baptist Chapel in Leicester, his new, dynamic evangelism soon led to conversions but not always the approval of the deacons. In his ministries at Regent's Park Chapel in London he reversed declining attendances and memberships. But it was at Melbourne Hall in Leicester and, twice, at Christ Church in London that he multiplied conversions and numbers.

When he departed from Melbourne Hall in 1887, he left not just a large membership and thriving church agencies but also a team of supporters who, with Meyer's successors, kept the church in this healthy position for the following decades. Christ Church was in dire straights when Meyer took over in 1892.

Congregations and income had fallen, the huge building was in need of repair, and enthusiasm seemed lacking. Within a few years, the Sunday services were usually full, the building was in good shape, conversions were common, and it had sufficient money not only to pay off debts but to finance expansion.

According to both Meyer and Turner, the most significant gains at Christ Church were the drawing in of working class people and their integration with the usual middle class attenders. Charles Booth reported on Turner's enthusiasm about the P.S.A. Brotherhood, 'At the start, efforts were made to keep out those who were going to any place of worship and Mr. Turner says that with few exceptions those who have joined have been non-church goers, and mostly of the roughest class of working men: they are drawn from an area of about a mile from the church.' He continued, 'Meyer has developed a spirit of camaraderie [handwriting not clear] between rich and poor which before was unknown.'

Christ Church became so well-known that visits from journalists and Christians from abroad were frequent. Their interest was aroused because Christ Church was bucking a national trend. Peter Shepherd points out that 'The vitality and growth of Nonconformity, such a dramatic feature of English society ... was in decline from mid-century onwards.'

No doubt, Meyer's preaching was a major means of building up the church. But he had other talents or skills. One, already discussed, was his ability to recruit helpers and his capacity to communicate with people of all classes. Another was his skill as a personal worker. He considered neighbourhood visiting to be essential. Street, who knew him well, said he 'often paid nearly a score of pastoral visits in a day; and because of his intense interest in people he had a wonderfully exact knowledge of their family affairs, and was appealed to in every crisis.' People spoke of his sympathy for and tenderness to those families he came across in the back streets of Leicester and London.

This concern also applied to church members. He once wrote. 'It is not enough to preach to the flock once or twice each week. There must be personal supervision; watching for souls as by those who must give account; seeking them if they go astray; tracking them to the precipice down which they have fallen; and never resting until the straying sheep is brought again to the fold.' He would go to enormous lengths to help individuals. In his Leicester days, he preached one evening in Northampton and declined the offer of overnight hospitality. He insisted on hurrying back to Leicester to be with a man who had backslidden into heavy drinking. In another case, he gave hours to a regular at Christ Church who confessed that he had committed a serious crime in New York. Meyer counselled him to go to the police and eventually he was jailed in New York. Later Meyer visited him there and found him in good spirits.

Meyer was a superb organiser. He insisted on being the head of the multitude of agencies within his churches. This did not mean he ran them on a day-to-day basis but rather that each had a committee which kept him informed. The committees also appointed representatives which came to a council chaired by Meyer and which considered the directions and programmes of each body. He advised that the minister be personally acquainted with the minutest details, including 'the boiler used at the great tea meetings' and that he be prepared to 'shift the forms for a meeting, dust seats, light a fire and see to the boiling water'. He was very much the leader of his churches but a leader who was not distant from the workers. His rare mixture of skills contributed to their large growth.

The Social Activist

Inside and outside of church, Meyer was also a social activist. At Melbourne Hall and Christ Church and, to a lesser extent at Regent's Park, he established a large number of social agencies. Moreover, at Christ Church, he did not have the advantage of a rich church to fund them. The wealthy congregation at the Metropolitan Tabernacle meant that Spurgeon always had the money for his large children's home and other enterprises. By contrast, Meyer wrote of Christ Church, 'There are no millionaires but ... the bulk of the people have got simply the necessaries of life.' He added that the self-restraint and frugality required of his members in order to give, released a greater power.

The criticism used to be heard that evangelicals in Victorian times were too spiritually minded to be concerned with the worldly needs of others. Kathleen Heasman, in her study, remedies this view by instancing numbers of voluntary organisations which were initiated by concerned evangelicals. None the less, David Bebbington, a leading scholar of evangelicalism, makes three important points. First, many evangelicals were reluctant to participate in any social involvement. William Wilberforce and Lord Shaftesbury, he says, 'were exceptional figures'. Second, where they were active it tended to be against 'social sins', such as impurity and intemperance. These sins were hindrances to people becoming Christians. Third, few seemed motivated by compassion for the poor. He gives the example that their indignation over the employment of women and children underground stemmed more from reports that they were 'lowered to work down mineshafts together half-naked'. To be fair, Heasman does identify some compassionate evangelicals. Fourth, evangelicals showed little interest in structural reforms. They might run soup kitchens but did not want political action to remove the causes of poverty. As Bebbington argues, evangelicals tended to be conservative both spiritually and politically.

Heasman agrees that the evangelicals were rarely involved in political reform and adds that few advocated the passing of liquor licensing laws and took little interest in Educational Acts. She explains that they preferred to carry out their relief work through separate voluntary agencies set up for the purpose rather than through the churches. Where their churches were involved, it was through mission churches which maintained the distance between the social classes. She acknowledges that, although evangelicals have not been given sufficient credit for their efforts, their organisations reached a peak in the 1860s and 1870s and then gradually declined.

Meyer too was an evangelical. His social outreach was essentially church based. He was not the only evangelical to do this but his work was unusually extensive. His right hand man, Turner, told Charles Booth, 'The work of this church is probably the biggest thing of its kind in London.' At Leicester, Providence House was a lodging house and workshop which could not be contained within Melbourne Hall, which was full of other activities. Likewise at Christ Church, some clubs had to be located outside, although always in the immediate neighbourhood. But Meyer's priority was the church as the hub of social action. He disliked missions because they separated social action from the church and did not break down the barriers between rich and poor. Locating it within the church not only promoted social integration, it also drew working class people nearer to the sound of the gospel. This successful bringing together of social welfare, class integration and evangelism was an outstanding feature of Meyer's work.

Of course, Meyer did want working class people to be converted. But he was also driven by a deep compassion for the plight of those known as the abject poor. He insisted that help be given to the most needy simply because they were in deep distress and not as a bait to draw them into the church. He was deeply moved by the lives of vulnerable young women, of wives treated badly by men, and widows left without support. Their conditions provoked within him a mixture of sadness at their enforced poverty and anger that it was not relieved by those who had the means. Yet, while seeing the vulnerability of poor people, while acknowledging that numbers then opted for evil and immoral life styles, Meyer was also unusual in having a respect for those at the lower end of society. He praised the hard work in gruelling conditions of many manual workers, he drew attention to the budgeting skills and self-sacrifice of wives and mothers, and he identified the abilities and willingness to help of men and women after a long, hard day at the factory or home.

Being so close to poverty and social deprivation, Meyer realised that some poor people not only disliked the harshness and stigma of the Poor Law, they also disliked being treated as objects of charity. Next, he perceived that the free market economy drove some people into poverty by low wages and unemployment over which its victims had no control. He increasingly accepted the need for structural changes within society, that is, government intervention to help. He sympathised with the growing Labour Party, especially its emphasis on people acting together, but he never accepted socialism. Instead he sided with a Liberal Party which itself became a reforming party. Meyer agreed with state provision of unemployment pay and pensions and, indeed, went further than most in his calls for better pay for women. Few conservative evangelicals articulated these policies. Indeed some considered that they were the same as socialism and would make individuals too reliant on the state. However, Meyer always insisted that the relief of poverty was rooted in the gospel and that state provision enhanced the dignity of down-trodden people. He added that it would never replace the important place of voluntary and church social agencies and of individual charity.

Meyer joined with other evangelicals in national societies which campaigned for temperance and purity. In contrast to some, he also called for state action to limit licensing hours (and to close some vendors who broke existing rules) and for local authorities to use existing legislation to close brothels. When the authorities replied that they had no evidence, Meyer and his colleagues undertook to get it.

The nineteenth century was an age of expansion of voluntary societies which contributed to the development of modern social work. The names of many of their leaders are still known today – Thomas Barnardo, George Muller and Thomas Bowman Stephenson for their children's homes, Elizabeth Fry for her work with prisoners, Mary Carpenter for helping young offenders and many more. Yet few if any books on voluntary agencies or social work make mention of Meyer. The reason is probably that he did not found a national society, did not want his name attached to a large institution. Rather he concentrated on initiating a number of varied and smaller initiatives in one area or district. In this sense he was an unacknowledged forerunner of modern neighbourhood work in which the emphasis is on providing local facilities, encouraging residents to be involved in running them, and strengthening the sense of community.

Not only did Meyer initiate services, support welfare reforms, and call for tighter legislation, he also participated in passive resistance to oppose the Education Act and later publicly supported the Liberal Party. There were Christian MPs but Meyer never considered this for himself. He became a political creature as a minister who claimed that his stance was an expression of his faith. There were some – including the Baptist John Clifford and the Wesleyan Hugh Price Hughes – but very few evangelicals of his kind.

A common criticism of ministers who become involved in welfare and politics is that their social gospel displaces their spiritual gospel. That accusation could not be levelled at Meyer who simultaneously proclaimed the atoning death of Christ, whose talks and books were all about holiness, and who increasingly foresaw the imminent return of Jesus Christ. Further, he refused to accept the division between the social and the spiritual gospels. When he encouraged Christians 'to endeavour to transfer as much as possible of our Lord's teaching to the Statute Book of the Nation', he did so not in a political speech but in the midst of his book about Christian living called *The Dedicated Life.*

Herein is one of the significant achievements of Meyer's ministry – his capacity to be spiritual, evangelical, socially involved and political. This, in conjunction with his personal friendliness with a range of Christians, helped to modify any splits within the evangelical camp. In the nineteen-twenties, some evangelicals, disappointed with the war and its aftermath, tended to withdraw into a personal and insular Christianity which wanted to shut out efforts to improve the world socially and materially. Meyer continued to support social action and still held their respect.

What Was He Like?
It is not easy to write fully about Meyer's family relationships as his personal diaries were destroyed, at his request, as soon as he died. In his publications, he did write about his childhood and

it is clear that he had a close relationship with his parents all through his life. They appeared to visit him often while he was at Melbourne Hall and where his father's fine bass voice was appreciated by the choir. It was during this period that both his parents died, his mother in 1884 and his father two years later.

Meyer also kept in touch with his three sisters. The Christ Church magazine of 1907 noted that one of them had become the honorary superintendent of the YWCA Servants' Home in Brighton. After he fainted in the pulpit in 1913, he convalesced with his sisters. One of them was with him during his last days and Meyer, though so ill, was anxious that she be given a cup of tea.

The nature of the relationship between Meyer and his wife, Jeannie, and daughter, Hilda, is difficult to understand . However, the following points can be made with some confidence. First, in his voluminous writings, Meyer makes few mentions of them. For instance, his wife accompanied him on his trip to South Africa, which he considered of such importance that he published a book about it as soon as he got back to Britain. It might have been expected that he would have recorded her impressions of the people they met and the social occasions they attended. Yet he refers to Jeannie only twice and then almost in passing. Again, he rarely if ever drew upon the experiences of his daughter to illustrate points in his sermons and writings – certainly other preachers often like talking about their children.

Second, the Meyers spent considerable periods apart. Sometimes he went abroad for weeks or months without his wife while he constantly travelled all over Britain, leaving her at home. While in Leicester, Jeannie and Hilda spent a winter in Cannes leaving Meyer to spend Christmas on his own. He seems to have enjoyed it and wrote glowingly about yuletide at Providence House. In 1885, three years before Meyer left Leicester, Jeannie and Hilda moved to London. Fullerton commented, 'The home was broken up and Meyer went into rooms.' While at Christ Church, Meyer had 'ensuite' facilities installed and spent much of his weekends there.

Third, Fullerton records an incident of 1900 sent to him by a doctor who had sought counselling from Meyer over a problem. During their interview, Meyer suddenly said with fervour, 'I have had a cross to bear in my life, and it has made me the man I am.' Fullerton, perplexingly, draws no conclusions from this but the implication is that it was to do with Meyer's personal relationships.

Fourth, in his will, Meyer left no money to his relatives.

Some of this suggests an unsatisfactory marriage and Randall states of the family, 'Relationships do not seem to have been close. Neither did Meyer appear to have an especially close relationship with his wife ... it seems that Jeannie showed relatively little interest in sharing in his ministry. In his later years it was not unknown for him to return from his Sunday preaching to his house to find a bridge party presided over by his wife.' This must have been galling to Meyer who, in one of his books, condemns card playing as a waste of time.

Yet there is another side. In 1900, a reporter recorded a part of Meyer's sermon at Christ Church in which he was talking about the relationship between husband and wife. Meyer said, 'The love and faithfulness of my wife for thirty years have a bigger claim on me than the new love of the honeymoon. If you begin to treat your wife with tenderness and consideration, she will think of you.' He concluded with, 'I have kept my text to the end. The gentleman who married us gave our text at the marriage altar. It is this, "Be ye kind one to another, tenderhearted, forgiving one another, even as God for Christ's sake hath forgiven you" (Eph. 4:32).'

Jennie Street, who appeared to be close to the family, wrote, 'Mrs Meyer has ever sought to participate in her husband's public work, and perhaps few who profit by Mr. Meyer's preaching and writing realise that they owe some thanks to the wife who has cared for his home and set him free for outside engagements.'

She also revealed that, in Leicester, Mrs Meyer did lead a Bible Class until she became so ill that doctors ordered her to spend a winter with her daughter in the south of France. This explains why the Meyers were apart one Christmas. While away, Jeannie wrote long letters to her Bible Class members saying, 'I love to think how many loving ones are praying for me. ... I miss you all very much. But my spirit is ever present with you at the class on Sunday afternoons, and I pray that you may have a rich blessing.'

Fullerton, in addition to his comments already cited, added that, after Hilda married and had children, the Meyers were "greatly attached" to their grandchildren.' It was Fullerton who pointed out that, when the former Barnardo boy from America, by then a minister, came to Britain it was both the Meyers who gave him warm hospitality. And it was Fullerton who explained that, 'owing to indifferent health she (Mrs Meyer) never took much share in his work of ministry'. Her illness, which is never named, was crucial. It prompted the Meyers to move from York to Leicester and when that city's climate was also unsuitable this was a contributory factor in their move to London.

For much of the time, her affliction seemed to confine Jeannie to the house. Perhaps, as she could rarely go to church, she did develop interests inside the home like card playing with friends. But this did not mean that the Meyers' love for and respect for each other was impaired. Twenty-eight years after their wedding, Meyer penned a dedication in his book *Gospel of John: the light and life of man: love to the uttermost*, writing, 'This book on THE UTTERMOST LOVE OF CHRIST is dedicated to my dear wife, whose patient care of our home has enabled me to write so much and travel so far in His service.'

Of course, Jeannie was never an Amy Shakespeare who was a leader alongside her husband during John Howard Shakespeare's pastorate in Norwich, and who supported and accompanied him when he became secretary of the Baptist Union. In 1905, leading Baptists presented her with £50 'to be spent in utter selfishness' as a token of their appreciation. When Shakespeare wrote to persuade Meyer to go to Regent's Park Chapel, he added, 'I trust my wife's judgment very much in these matters' and she too urged this path on Meyer. But Amy was an exceptionable woman whose husband suffered ill-health. Jeannie was a more ordinary woman who herself was frequently ill. Perhaps the cross Meyer had to bear was the illness which restricted his wife. This did not mean they had an unsatisfactory marriage.

Whatever his relationships at home, Meyer enjoyed a wide circle of friends. Most of them seemed to be active Christians, including families who gave him hospitality and ministerial colleagues. Enid Measures from Derbyshire told me that her grandfather, a Baptist minister, and his wife were friends of Meyer's and that they had a photo of him in the family photo album and had retained a Christmas card from him. He did not appear to engage in leisure activities with his friends, apart from long walks and conversations. Indeed, his only relaxation was reading, apart from sightseeing and hill-climbing when on holidays and tours. In his unpublished *Memories of a Long Life*, Meyer lists a number of people of whom he spoke warmly as friends. Amongst the most treasured were Hudson Taylor and Dwight Moody. John Howard Shakespeare was certainly one of his closest colleagues, although they disagreed over some matters. They enjoyed working together when Meyer was president of the Baptist Union and Meyer did discuss his plans for the future with John Howard and probably with his wife.

As well as having friends, Meyer had a friendly even playful manner. He enjoyed the company of young people, was full of life at the Bank holiday walks, and was always happy when in the company of his beloved working class women at Christ Church. He declared that laughter was one of God's great gifts. Meyer may have been a devout man but he was not a dull one.

As a former employee of a city firm, it is not surprising that Meyer was careful about money – other people's money. Charities and societies valued him as a committee member because he understood accounts and was adept at raising funds. Yet he never worried about his own finances. Some Victorian ministers in fashionable churches enjoyed large salaries and lived in some style. Street states that Meyer did receive financially tempting offers which he always declined. When he moved from Regent's Park to Christ Church, he took a considerable drop in salary.

Shakespeare said that at Christ Church 'he has been content with a small salary'.

Frequently, Meyer had to support his expanding work out of his own pocket. Certainly he did in Leicester and Christ Church. The local campaigns against brothels were financed almost entirely by him. He did all this from the proceeds of his publications. Meyer did not talk about the extent of his generosity and it was Jennie Street who revealed that he kept a separate account for these earnings and that he devoted 'every penny earned by his pen to the work he has felt called to carry on without appealing to his fellow-men for financial aid.'

He also gave to individuals. In his writings, Meyer counselled Christians not to waste their money on so-called loafers. His own practice could be different and one close friend pointed out that he could not resist the appeal of anyone who was down and out. If there was doubt about the case, Meyer's response was 'better to be let down occasionally than never to have the satisfaction of lending a helping hand.'

He was always confident that God would meet his needs. One day he lent a man £5 to buy a share in a fish and chip shop and then realised he had no more money left and was shortly to start a train journey costing £3 for the fare. He was not worried and opened the day's mail. The first letter contained five one pound notes from somebody to whom he had previously made a loan. He wrote, 'In my life I have found repeatedly that in proportion as I have given I have gotten, and that men have given into my bosom, according to heaven's own measure, pressed down, heaped up, and running over.'

It must be asked what were Meyer's faults and limitations? It is difficult to get at these from publications written by his admirers. But Meyer himself admitted that he was prone to be jealous of other speakers, especially when they received greater praise and larger attendances than himself. He once wrote that 'Christian ministers are proud of their influence, and sermons, and the admiration they receive' and he may well have been including himself in their number. John Pollock in his history of Keswick thought that Meyer – whom he never met – exaggerated his own part in the rise of the Convention and calls him 'a curiously childlike egoist'.

Yet Meyer was not the man to push himself to the front. He shared platforms with prime ministers and archbishops but he never sought their company, never tried to worm his way into the establishment, never hankered after honours. He certainly did not cultivate the friendship of the titled members of Regent's Park. If anything the opposite was true. He stated that 'God is down here among common folk' and that is where Christians should be. He often repeated that God's most glorious deeds were done not by the wealthy but by people like John Carey, a cobbler, and John Bunyan, a tinker. Anyone who reads his many writings will sense that he was happiest amongst the working class people at Leicester and Christ Church.

Fullerton tells that when Meyer got bored at rambling committee meetings, he would open his case, get out some letters and get on with his correspondence. Understandable but hardly polite.

No doubt, Meyer was sometimes jealous and proud but he acknowledges these weaknesses and, over the years, seemed to master them. Even Pollock conceded that Meyer's personality had 'a winsomeness' that made him one of the best loved of all the second generation of Keswick speakers.

A further criticism is that he did depart from some churches abruptly and with insufficient regard for the officials and members he left behind. His several moves between churches contrasts with one of his friends, John Wilson of Woolwich. Wilson was minister of Woolwich Baptist Tabernacle for over fifty years and built up a large, working class church with many welfare agencies in a very deprived area. By staying so long, Wilson knew families through several generations, trained young people to become long-serving helpers, and became a respected figure to Woolwich people from all ranks of life. Meyer had reasons for his moves such as the poor health of his wife, his desire to work with the masses, and to have a Baptist base when he travelled the country for the

Baptist Union. None the less, as a community worker whose policy was to live long-term where I worked, I wonder if Meyer would have achieved even more by staying longer in a smaller number of churches.

Ordinary Man and Gentleman

In some ways Meyer was a very ordinary person. He experienced no dramatic conversion. He did not shine at school or college in studies or sport. In appearance and dress, he did not stand out in a crowd. Yet he sought to be close to God. He always started the day with prayers but not long ones, for he used to say that he had eternity in which to adore God. Yet he frequently prayed as he went about his daily round. Due to preach at Hitchin, he once jumped on a train only to find that the first stop was Peterborough. He went down on his knees and told God. The train slowed down at Hitchin and Meyer jumped out. His prayer time was followed by Bible study for at least a half hour. Meyer always sought to learn from other Christians and to deepen his own spirituality. He was prepared to follow Moody's emphasis on evangelism, to consecrate his life under C. T. Studd, to receive the filling of the Holy Spirit by faith at Keswick, to identify himself with Christ's death when in South Africa, and to commit himself to missionary expansion late in life. He rarely stood still physically or spiritually and so this ordinary man became an extra-ordinary Christian.

I find this encouraging. The stories of giants like John Wesley, George Muller and Hudson Taylor can inspire yet over-awe us. I see a photo of Meyer's slight figure, waiting at the railway station, wearing his usual homburg hat and carrying his brolly and brief case and I feel I can identify with him. If he could become an extra-ordinary servant of God so can many other ordinary folk.

But he was also a gentleman. I do not mean gentleman in the Victorian sense of the well-to-do man well-versed in etiquette. As a boy, I went to cricket at Lords to see the Gentlemen against the Players. The former were amateurs who could afford to spend the summer playing cricket and, in their Oxbridge blazers, would not enter the same dressing rooms as the Players. The latter earned their living by playing. They won.

By a gentleman or gentlewoman, I mean persons who display the qualities of gentleness. Jesus was a gentle person who showed compassion for the needy, who focussed on troubled individuals with tenderness, and who took on the role of a servant. This did not mean He was not a leader nor that He neglected justice. As was foretold in Isaiah 42:3, 'He will be gentle – He will not shout or raise His voice in public. ... He will bring full justice to all who have been wronged.' The apostle Paul encouraged all Christians to 'Pursue a godly life, along with faith, love, perseverance and gentleness' (1 Tim. 6:11). He said that the requirements for Christian leaders were to be 'gentle, peace loving, and not one who loves money' (1 Tim. 3:3).

Meyer was a gentle person. He frequently exhorted Christians to be gentle. He pointed out that not only was Jesus gentle but so too was Paul. The great apostle could sometimes be hot with indignation but mostly he was 'winsome and gentle' among his converts. He added that Paul 'never lost the savour of the meekness and gentleness of Christ'. He said that gentleness was a part of practical godliness and that, in general, all servants of God must 'be gentle unto all'. In particular, he encouraged men to be gentle towards their wives. He wrote, 'But let men be more thoughtful and tender. When they feel most put out and irritated, either with or without cause, it would be well to force themselves to bridge yawning chasms at once by a caress. ... No woman would do for pay what thousands are doing for love. They ask no other wage than tenderness, which is the expression of a true and honest affection.' As a Keswick speaker, Meyer often spoke on the gifts of the Spirit – and one of these is gentleness.

He practised what he preached and there are many mentions of his attentiveness, thoughtfulness, tenderness and sympathy. One of his oldest members was suffering a deep depression when he saw her in church. Returning to his vestry, he immediately wrote her a letter of comfort which strengthened her. Speaking at a large meeting with General William Booth, Meyer noticed there was just one boy present and he was pumping the organ (hard work, I've done it myself). Afterwards, Meyer sought him out to bless him – which the boy remembered all his life. In the USA, his friend Tydeman Chilvers arrived very late when the Conference Hall was closed. Meyer had waited up for him, found some tea and toast, said his friend was too tired to pray and, after praying himself, guided him to his room. On a crowded tram car, he did not stand up but squeezed along to make room for a standing woman. He apologised for not giving her his seat and explained that the last time he did so the tram was so full that he got kicked off and was late for his meeting. Meyer received an enormous number of letters, often from people who had read his books and wanted help. He insisted on answering every one in person, no matter how tired he was.

Writing for Christians, Meyer urged them, 'to have a sympathetic ear, and to make room in our heart for the story of human pain, sorrow, and loneliness, which some, who are comparative strangers, may want to confide in us.' The numbers who turned to him – and he gives examples in his books about Melbourne Hall and Christ Church – showed that needy people recognised his willingness to help.

Meyer, in his book *Religion in Homespun,* ended with a chapter on 'True Gentle-Folk'. He picked out 'a keen sensitiveness for the feelings of others' as a characteristic of Gentle-Folk. It was a quality he had. He possessed an almost inexhaustible patience with people who demanded his attention. Likewise he rarely seemed to get irritated. A woman who sometimes typed for him somehow lost two of his articles so that he had to do them again. She was very upset but Meyer simply wrote to her, 'I can imagine your distress. I think it was a good thing as my second attempt was an improvement.' Indeed, it was so rare for him to show displeasure that Chester Mann felt bound to record that, near the end of his life, he almost resented being offered help as he went up stairs.

One journalist reported that he had heard sneers that Meyer was 'shallow and sugary'. Having met him, he decided that this was a wrong judgment and commented on his 'gentleness of motives and ability to sympathise with others'. Another and well-known journalist, Raymond Blathwayt, wrote, 'He is a man of sympathy, understanding, and of remarkable power and capacity for uplifting and encouraging the weary and the broken-hearted. You instinctively realise that he is a man who would never break the bruised reed, nor quench the smoking flax, which is, perhaps, the highest qualification, as it is one of the rarest, that a minister of God can possess.'

These qualities did not mean that Meyer was a softie. He faced threats of violence, opposition from publicans and brothel owners, and criticisms in the press. He did not neglect the pursuit of justice. He expressed the whole of the Biblical concept of gentleness. The Christian scholar, Alec Motyer, concluded that, even in Christian circles, we tend to admire the more extrovert and pushy leaders. He continues that, if offered a gift, few would choose 'a gentle and quiet spirit'. Yet gentleness is an attractive quality and one that Christians need to display in an increasingly aggressive, noisy and selfish culture. Meyer was nicknamed 'St. Francis with a Bradshaw'. We need more gentle people like him, although not necessarily with the railway guide.

Post Script

Early in the Second World War, Upton Chapel in Lambeth Road was destroyed by bombs. Christ Church was damaged but left standing. Upton Chapel had a minister but no building while Christ Church had a building but no minister. The two churches joined forces at Christ Church.

After the war, Christ Church was assessed to be damaged beyond repair, although the Lincoln Tower remained intact. The church was re-built and re-opened in 1960. It included a large stained glass window depicting a number of Christian characters, one of whom is F. B. Meyer. Hawkstone Hall was re-designed in the nineteen-seventies. The church of Upton Chapel and Christ Church became part of the Congregational Union but retained a Baptist ideology with a baptistry.

By 2003, the membership was down to twenty and the church asked the Oasis Trust to develop a new church under the leadership of its Baptist minister, Steve Chalke. Founded in 1986, Oasis has been in partnership with another evangelical agency, Faithworks, since 2001. Oasis has developed a large number of community and youth projects in Southwark, Croydon, Greenwich, Leeds and Birmingham while Faithworks supports and stimulates Christian and social services throughout the UK. In 2004, the Revd Malcolm Duncan took over the leadership of Faithworks, while recently Dave Steell has become senior minister of what is now called church.co.uk. Steve Chalke pursues a wider ministry throughout the country and is the network leader of churches and groups, especially in deprived areas, which subscribe to the Faithworks' basis of faith. Together Oasis, Faithworks and church.co.uk run a combination of preaching, church building and social action which has much in common with the ministry of Frederick Brotherton Meyer on the same location and in the same neighbourhood just over one hundred years ago.

SOURCES

The Christ Church Archives
Meyer retained a large amount of material which I have sorted under the following headings.

1. Certificates
A number of certificates (or copies) relating to Meyer's birth, marriage, family and education.

2. His Mother's Notes
Mrs Meyer's handwritten memoir headed 'Early Life of Fritz. Notes by his fondly attached mother.'

3. Meyer's Early Note
A few handwritten pages written by Meyer on 14 March 1864 concerning his call to the ministry.

4. Letters
a. Thirty-one handwritten letters from Meyer to his friend Herbert, probably between 1865–1869.

b. Handwritten letters from ministerial friends giving him advice about his future.

c. At Christ Church, large numbers of letters to and from Meyer concerning people leaving or joining the church between 1892–1894.

d. Letters by and to Meyer – some typewritten – concerning his appointments to and resignations from churches.

e. Letters from Meyer to the body of church members.

f. Various other letters.

g. Letters of condolences and tributes following Meyer's death in 1929.

5. Magazines and Journals

Meyer extracted from magazines and journals, articles by himself or about himself. They were taken from the following, *The Baptist Times, The British Monthly, The British Weekly, The Chimney Corner, The Christian, The Christian Age, The Christian Commonwealth, The Christian Endeavour Times, The Christian Herald and Signs of Our Times, The Christian Leader, The Christian Treasury, The Christian World, The Daily News, Daybreak, The Freechurchman, Great Thoughts, The Home Magazine, The Life of Faith, The Manchester Guardian, The New York Observer, The Onslow Herald, The Portal, The Quiver, Social Service, The Sunday Companion, The Sunday Express, The Sunday Magazine, The Sunday Reader, The Sunday School Chronicle and Christian Outlook, The Sunday School World, The Sunday Strand, The Tribune, The Westminster Record, World and Work.*

6. Untitled Magazines and Journals

Meyer had cut out articles from twenty-six magazines or journals but did not retain their title.

7. Cuttings

A further 742 press cuttings are made up of newspaper and journal coverage of events in which Meyer participated, of reports of his talks, of happenings at Christ Church, and of reports which Meyer wrote while abroad and sent for publication.

8. Christ Church Magazine

There are two complete sets of the Christ Church Magazine for 1895 and 1898 and individual copies for December 1894, February 1897, December 1900, May 1903, March 1906, and July 1907.

9. Programmes and Leaflets

A number of programmes of meetings in which Meyer was a speaker and a small number of leaflets which advertised forthcoming meetings.

10. Rowland Hill Almshouses

A bound copy of the handwritten minutes of the Rowland Hill Almshouses.

11. Photographs

A number of photographs, mainly of Meyer and his family.

12. Additional Items

a. A pamphlet entitled *The Revd F. B. Meyer, B.A., Minister of Christ Church, Westminster Bridge Road, London,* London, Hodder & Stoughton, 1905. The author is not stated but it is either Meyer himself – and it contains photographs of his parents which he had at hand – or the journalist and writer Jennie Street, who knew Meyer well.

b. Pages which consist of press cuttings of reports mainly written by Meyer, about Keswick, his trips to the USA and elsewhere, his friends, and the Welsh Revival. It is entitled *Memories of a Long Life* and may have been the basis of a book which was never completed.

c. A pamphlet headed *The Christ Church Jubilee Year Book 1926* which celebrates the history of the church. It is arranged by John Reed and has a part written by Meyer.

Books by F. B. Meyer

The following are the books written by Meyer which have informed this study. For a fuller list of his numerous publications see the bibliography in Ian Randall's book.

Abraham: Or the Obedience of Faith, London, Morgan & Scott, 1894.

The Art of Life, London, National Council of the Evangelical Free Churches, Morgan & Scott, 1905.

The Bells of Is: Or Voices of Human Need and Sorrow, London, Morgan & Scott, 1894.

The Best of F. B. Meyer, Fearn, Ross-shire, Christian Focus Publications, 1994.

Blessed Are Ye, London, Sunday School Union, 1898.

The Book of Common Prayer. The Grounds of Religious Nonconformity, London, S. W. Partridge, no date.

The Call and Challenge of the Unseen, Toronto, Canada, Missions of Biblical Education, 1927.

Cavalry to Pentecost, London, Marshall Brothers, no date.

Cecil Robertson of Sianfu, London, Carey Press, second edition, 1916.

Cheers for Life's Pilgrimage, New York, Fleming H. Revell Co., 1897.

Christ in Isaiah, London, Marshall & Scott, 1895.

Christian Living, London, Morgan & Scott, 1888.

The Creed of Creeds, London, Sir Issac Pitman & Sons, 1906.

David: Shepherd, psalmist, king, London, Morgan & Scott, 1895.

The Dedicated Life, London, National Council of the Evangelical Free Churches, 1904.

The Directory of the Devout Life, London, National Council of the Evangelical Free Churches, 1904.

Elijah and the secret of his power, London, Morgan & Scott, 1888.

Epistle to the Philippians: a devotional commentary, London, The Religious Tract Society, third impression, 1906.

Exodus I-XX v. 17, London, The Religious Tract Society, no date.

Expository Preaching Plan and Methods, London, Morgan & Scott, 1888.

Five 'Musts' of the Christian Life and Other Sermons, London, Morgan & Scott, 1928.

Foreword to F. S. Clayton, *John Wilson of Woolwich*, London, Kingsgate Press, 1928.

For Me and Thee, London, Walter G. Wheeler & Co., 1903.

The Future Tenses of the Blessed Life, London, Morgan & Scott, 1894.

Gospel of John: the light and life of man: love to the uttermost, London, Oliphants, First Lakeland Edition, 1970.

Great Verses Through the Bible: a devotional commentary on key verses, London, Marshall, Morgan & Scott, new edition, 1977.

A Holy Temple, London, Morgan & Scott, 1894.

In Defence of the Faith, London, S. W. Partridge, 1911.

In the Beginning God! London, S. C. Brown, Langham & Co., 1904.

I Promise, Boston, USA, United Society of Christian Endeavour, 1899.

Israel: A prince with God: the story of Jacob re-told, London, Morgan & Scott, no date.

Jeremiah: Priest and prophet, London, Morgan & Scott, 1894.

John the Baptist, London, Morgan & Scott, 1900.

Joseph: Beloved, hated, exalted, London, Morgan & Scott, 1891.

Key Words of the Inner Life: Studies in the epistle to the Ephesians, London, Morgan & Scott, 1893.

The Majesty of Conscience, London, National Labour Press, 1917.

Moses: the servant of God, London, Marshall, Morgan & Scott, New Edition, 1953.

Our Daily Walk, Fearn, Ross-shire, Christian Focus, reprinted 1998.

Paul: a servant of Jesus Christ, London, Morgan & Scott, 1897.

Peter: Fisherman, Disciple, Apostle, London, Morgan & Scott, 1919.

The Prophet of Hope: Studies in Zechariah, London, Morgan & Scott, reprinted 1961.

Religion in Homespun, London, Isbister & Co., 1903.

Reveries and Realities: Or Life and Work in London, London, Morgan & Scott, 1896.

Saved and Kept, London, Morgan & Scott, 1897.

The Secret of Guidance, Chicago, Moody Press, no date.

Seven Reasons for Believer's Baptism, London, J. Vice, 1882.

Seven Reasons for Joining a Church, London, J. Vice, no date.

The Shepherd Psalm, Fearn, Ross-shire, Christian Focus Publications, new edition, 2005.

Some Secrets of Christian Living, London, Marshall, Morgan & Scott, new edition, 1953.

The Soul's Ascent, London, Horace, Marshall & Son, 1904.

The Soul's Pure Intention, London, Samuel Bagster & Son, 1906.

The Soul's Wrestle With Doubt, London, National Council of Evangelical Free Churches, 1905.

Tried By Fire: Expositions of the First Epistle of Peter, Pennsylvania, USA, revised edition, 1993.

The Way Into the Holiest: expositions of the Epistle to the Hebrews, London, Morgan & Scott, 1893.

A Winter in South Africa, London, National Council of the Evangelical Free Churches, 1908.

Other Books and Articles

A. J. Arnold, *Jubilee of the Evangelical Alliance: Proceedings of the Tenth International Conference Held in London 1896,* London, Shaw & Co., 1897.

BBC, *The Romantics*, London, Open University, 2005.

D. Bebbington, *Holiness in Nineteenth Century England*, Carlisle, The Paternoster Press, 2000.

D. Bebbington, 'Evangelicals, Theology and Social Transformation' in D. Hilborn (ed), *Movement for Change. Evangelical Perspectives on Social Transformation*, Carlisle, Paternoster Press, 2004.

C. Booth, *Life and Labour of the People of London*, vol. 1, London, Williams & Norgate, 1889.

W. Booth, *In Darkest England and The Way Out*, London, Salvation Army, 1890.

J. H. Y. Briggs, *The English Baptists of the Nineteenth Century*, Didcot, Baptist Historical Society, 1994.

A. J. Broomhall, *The Shaping of Modern China: Hudson Taylor's Life and Legacy*, vols. 1 and 2, Carlisle, Piquant Editions, 2005.

A. Bryant, *English Saga 1840–1940*, London, Collins with Eyre & Spottiswoode, third impression, 1941.

C. Bryant, *Possible Dreams. A Personal History of the British Christian Socialists*, London, Hodder & Stoughton, 1996.

A. I. Calman, *Life and Labours of John Ashworth*, Manchester, Tubbs & Brook, 1875.

J. C. Carlile, *The Story of the English Baptists*, London, J. Clarke, 1905.

G. Dale, *God's Politicians. The Christian Contribution to 100 Years of Labour*, London, HarperCollins, 2000.

F. Engels, *The Condition of the Working Class in England*, London, Lawrence & Wishart, reprinted, 1984.

Sir R. Ensor, *England 1870–1914*, Oxford, Clarendon Press, reprinted 1966.

L. Fischer, *The Life of Mahatma Gandhi*, London, HarperCollins, reprinted, 1997.

W. Y. Fullerton, *F. B. Meyer: A Biography*, London, Marshall, Morgan & Scott, 1929.

E. Goold, 'The P.S.A. Movement' in R.Mudie-Smith (ed), *The Religious Life of London*, London, Hodder & Stoughton, 1904

N. Grubb, *C. T. Studd: Cricketer and Pioneer*, London, Religious Tract Society, 1936 edition.

M. Guldseth, *Streams: The Flow of Inspiration from Dwight Moody to Frank Buchman*, Fritz Creek, USA, Fritz Creek Studios, reprinted 1983.

M. A. Hamilton, *Arthur Henderson*, London, Heinemann Ltd., 1938.

G. Haw, *From Workhouse to Westminster. The Life Story of Will Crooks MP*, London, Cassell & Co., 1907.

K. Heaseman, *Evangelicals in Action: An Appraisal of their Social Work*, London, Geoffrey Bles, 1962.

B. Holman, *Good Old George: The Life of George Lansbury*, Oxford, Lion Publishing, 1990.

P. Houghton, *Amy Carmichael of Dohnavur*, London, S.P.C.K., 1959.

A. Hyde, *The First Blitz: The German Air Campaign Against Britain 1917–18*, Barnsley, Pen and Sword Books Ltd., 2002.

J. Jordan, *Josephine Butler*, London, John Murray, 2001.

J. Lake, *Christ Church and Upton Chapel 1783–1983* (pamphlet), London, 1983.

G. Lansbury, *My Life*, London, Constable, 1928.

T. Larsen, *Christabel Pankhurst: Fundamentalism and Feminism in Coalition*, Woodbridge, The Boydell Press, 2002.

G. Lean, *Frank Buchman: A Life*, London, Constable, 1985.

W. Major Scott, *Aspects of Christian Mysticism*, London, John Murray, 1907.

A. C. Mann, *F. B. Meyer: Preacher, Teacher, Man of God*, London, Allen & Unwin, 1929.

A. Marwick, *Clifford Allen: The Open Conspirator*, Edinburgh and London, Oliver and Boyd, 1964.

C. Masterman, 'The Problem of South London', in R. Mudie-Smith (ed), *op.cit.*

A. Mearns, *The Bitter Cry of Outcast London*, London, London Congregational Union, 1883.

A. Motyer, *The Message of James.* Leicester, Inter-Varsity Press, reprinted, 2003.

R. Mudie-Smith (ed), *The Religious Life of London, op. cit.*

C. Noel, *Socialism in Church History*, London, Frank Palmer, 1910.

C. Pankhurst, *The Lord Cometh: The World Crisis Explained*, London, Morgan & Scott, 1923.

E. Payne, *The Baptist Union: A Short History*, London, Kingsgate Press, 1959.

J. C. Pollock, *The Keswick Story*, London, Hodder & Stoughton, 1964.

J. C. Pollock, *Moody Without Sankey*, Fearn, Ross-shire, Christian Focus Publications, reprinted 2005.

F. Prochaska, *Christianity and Social Service in Modern Britain*, Oxford, Oxford University Press, 2006.

I. M. Randall, 'Spiritual Renewal and Social Awareness: Attempts to Develop Social Awareness in the Early Keswick Movement', *Vox Evangelica*, 23, 1993.

I. M. Randall, 'Incarnating the Gospel. Melbourne Hall, Leicester in the 1880s as a model for holistic ministry', *Baptist Quarterly*, 35, 1994.

I. M. Randall, *Spirituality and Social Change. The Contribution of F. B. Meyer (1847–1929)*, Carlisle, Paternoster Press, 2003.

I. M. Randall & D. Hilborn, *One Body in Christ. The History and Significance of the Evangelical Alliance*, Carlisle, Paternoster Press and Evangelical Alliance, 2001.

M. L. Rowlandson, *Life at the Keswick Convention*, Carlisle, OM Publishing, 1997.

B. Senior, *A Hundred Years at Surrey Chapel*, London, Passmore & Alabaster, 1892.

P. Shepherd, *The Making of a Modern Denomination: John Howard Shakespeare and the English Baptists, 1898–1924*, London, Paternoster Press, 2001.

H. F. Stevenson (ed), *Keswick's Triumphal Voice*, London, Marshall, Morgan & Scott, 1963.

M. J. Street, *F. B. Meyer: His Life and Work*, London, S. W. Partridge, 1902.

A. J. P. Taylor, *English History 1914–1945*, London, Penguin Books, reprinted 1987.

A. C. Underwood, *A History of the English Baptists*, Kingsgate Press, London, 1947.

T. Wilkinson Riddle, *The Faith of a Christian Mystic*, London, Marshall Brothers Ltd., 1914.

J. Wolffe (ed), *Evangelical Faith and Public Zeal. Evangelicals and Society in Britain 1780–1980*, London, S.P.C.K., 1995.

A. F. Young and E. T. Ashton, *British Social Work in the Nineteenth Century*, London, Routledge & Kegan Paul Ltd., second impression 1963.

J. Yuille, *The Homeless Children's Aid and Adoption Society*, (pamphlet), London, 1970.

Additional Material

C. Booth, 'Interview with Mr. H. Turner' (handwritten), July 19, 1899, Booth Collection, B271, London School of Economics Archives.

Christian Focus Publications
publishes books for all ages

Our mission statement –

STAYING FAITHFUL
In dependence upon God we seek to help make His infallible Word, the Bible, relevant. Our aim is to ensure that the Lord Jesus Christ is presented as the only hope to obtain forgiveness of sin, live a useful life and look forward to heaven with Him.

REACHING OUT
Christ's last command requires us to reach out to our world with His gospel. We seek to help fulfill that by publishing books that point people towards Jesus and help them develop a Christ-like maturity. We aim to equip all levels of readers for life, work, ministry and mission.

Books in our adult range are published in three imprints.
Christian Focus contains popular works including biographies, commentaries, basic doctrine and Christian living. Our children's books are also published in this imprint.
Mentor focuses on books written at a level suitable for Bible College and seminary students, pastors, and other serious readers. The imprint includes commentaries, doctrinal studies, examination of current issues and church history.
Christian Heritage contains classic writings from the past.

Christian Focus Publications, Ltd
Geanies House, Fearn, Ross-shire,
IV20 1TW, Scotland, United Kingdom
info@christianfocus.com

For details of our titles visit us on our website
www.christianfocus.com